D0552310

F4
27

HOW TO LOVE A DIFFICULT MAN

Nancy Good is a psychotherapist practising in New York. This is her first book.

Overcoming Common Problems Series

The ABC of Eating
Coping with anorexia, bulimia and
compulsive eating
JOY MELVILLE

Acne
How it's caused and how to cure it
PAUL VAN RIEL

An A–Z of Alternative Medicine
BRENT Q. HAFEN AND KATHRYN J.
FRANDSEN

Arthritis
Is your suffering really necessary?
DR WILLIAM FOX

Birth Over Thirty
SHEILA KITZINGER

Body Language
How to read others' thoughts by their gestures
ALLAN PEASE

Calm Down
How to cope with frustration and anger
DR PAUL HAUCK

Common Childhood Illnesses
DR PATRICIA GILBERT

Complete Public Speaker
GYLES BRANDRETH

Coping with Depression and Elation
DR PATRICK McKEON

Curing Arthritis Cookbook
Margaret Hills

Curing Arthritis – The Drug-free Way
MARGARET HILLS

Depression
DR PAUL HAUCK

Divorce and Separation
ANGELA WILLANS

The Epilepsy Handbook
SHELAGH McGOVERN

Everything You Need to Know About Adoption
MAGGIE JONES

Everything You Need to Know about Contact Lenses
DR ROBERT YOUNGSON

Everything You Need to Know about Your Eyes
DR ROBERT YOUNGSON

Everything You Need to Know About the Pill
WENDY COOPER AND TOM SMITH

Everything You Need to Know about Shingles
DR ROBERT YOUNGSON

Family First Aid and Emergency Handbook
DR ANDREW STANWAY

Fears and Phobias
What they are and how to overcome them
DR TONY WHITEHEAD

Feverfew
A traditional herbal remedy for migraine and
arthritis
DR STEWART JOHNSON

Fight Your Phobia and Win
DAVID LEWIS

Fit Kit
DAVID LEWIS

Flying Without Fear
TESSA DUCKWORTH AND DAVID
MILLER

Goodbye Backache
DR DAVID IMRIE WITH COLLEEN
DIMSON

How to Bring Up your Child Successfully
DR PAUL HAUCK

How to Control your Drinking
DRS W. MILLER AND R. MUNOZ

How to Cope with Stress
DR PETER TYRER

Overcoming Common Problems Series

Overcoming Common Problems Series

Overcoming Common Problems

HOW TO LOVE
A DIFFICULT MAN

Nancy Good

SHELDON PRESS
LONDON

First published in the USA in 1987 by St Martin's Press,
175 Fifth Avenue, New York, N.Y.

First published in Great Britain in 1987 by Sheldon Press
SPCK, Marylebone Road, London NW1 4DU

Grateful acknowledgement is made to the following for permission to reprint:

"I Go It Bad and That Ain't Good" by Duke Ellington and Paul Francis Webster.
Copyright © 1941, renewed 1969 Robbins Music Corporation. Rights assigned to
CBS Catalogue Partnership. All rights controlled and administered by CBS
Robbins Catalog, Inc. All rights reserved. International Copyright secured. Used
by permission.

Portions of "The Phoenix" by Judee Sill. 1973 Warner-Tamerlane Publishing
Corp. & Heart Food Music. All rights reserved. Used by permission.

Portions of "Kozmic Blues" by Janis Joplin. Copyright © 1970 Strong Arm
Music. All rights reserved. Reprinted by permission of the publisher.

Portions of "That's the Way I've Always Heard It Should Be" by Carly Simon
and Jacob Brackman. Carly Simon and Jacob Brackman, publishers. Used by
permission. All rights reserved.

Portions of "I Wanna Be Loved By You" by Bert Kalmar, Herbert Stothart and
Harry Ruby. 1928 (renewed) Warner Bros., Inc. and Harry Ruby Music Co. All
rights reserved. Used by permission.

"Reuben's Children" from *The Portable Dorothy Parker*. Copyright © 1928,
renewed © 1956 by Dorothy Parker. Reprinted by permission of Viking Penguin,
Inc.

British Library Cataloging in Publication Data

Good, Nancy
    How to love a difficult man.
    1. Men   2. Women   3. Interpersonal
    relations
    I. Title
    305.3   HQ1090

ISBN 0–85969–555–7

Printed in Great Britain by Biddles Limited, Guildford, Surrey

For my patients

Contents

Acknowledgements

This book would not have been written without the help, guidance, and expertise of many generous people. There were several colleagues who encouraged me. Among them is Dr. Lena Furgeri, who is always enthusiastic and who opened up my thoughts with her own courageous and challenging ideas about the conflicts between men and women. Mildred Moskowitz lent me her optimism and warm support, and gave me needed positive feedback on reading the book. Dr. Louis Ormont, who well knows the problems that love creates, said that I should write the book before I said I could. He unhesitatingly encouraged me to continue despite all stumbling blocks.

Then there are the people involved in shaping the manuscript and getting it published. I would never have met my agent, Agnes Birnbaum, if it weren't for Maryann Brinley, a talented writer interested in women's issues, who graciously provided the introduction. Agnes was equally important in the creative and business areas. She helped me mold my original vague ideas and was always there to explain the publishing industry. Agnes contacted Victoria Skurnick, who intuitively saw the need for this book. Vicki's comments and critiques helped to give the manuscript the direction and tone that it has. Toni Lopopolo, executive editor at St. Martin's, has been terrific in shepherding the book through its many stages to publication. Also at St. Martin's, Jack Caravela and Robin Desser were consistently patient, cheerful and bountiful sources of help and information. And Patty Romanowski provided important editorial assistance.

Finally, Wendell Craig, with whom I have lived for many years is, among his many talents, a computer wiz. He expertly guided me through the mysteries of word processing. Much more important, however, he continues to help me prove first hand that a relationship with a difficult but wonderful man is well worth the effort.

Foreword

No-one is perfect. Do I hear a cry of 'least of all men!' from the female gallery? We may spend years looking for the perfect man, encouraged by romantic fiction that 'Mr Right', who'll instinctively know what we want, must be out there somewhere. He isn't of course, just as there isn't the perfect woman. Once that's established and accepted, and you come across some not-so-perfect but likeable and even loveable men, you may decide to settle with one. That can be when the real difficulties start. If they're impossible, non-negotiable problems then you may decide to call it a day and put it down to experience. If so, then it's worth remembering that even pain can be profitable in the long run, we can learn and gain by mistakes. Being part of a heterosexual relationship, or part of a couple, are not the only tickets to a satisfying life anyway. However, if you decide to stay, to stick it out with a difficult man, how can you negotiate the maze?

Women are, on the whole, better trained to deal with emotions than men – at least, we're taught to deal with other peoples', though not necessarily our own. Little girls are trained to be mothers, and mothers take care, make sure that everyone is all right, and if they're not then fix it. They're taught to submerge their needs when others make demands, and woman can have real problems accepting their desires and difficulties are valid and acceptable. We are allowed to weep though. Little boys, on the other hand, are often encouraged to hide their tears, be strong, overcome their fears and lose their dependence on their mother. Some of that is quite healthy—for instance, perhaps more little girls could do with encouragement to conquer their fears and be adventurous—but some of it is terribly inhibiting.

Little boys can be told to grow up and not be soft, and then find that their softer and more vulnerable emotions which emerge in an intimate relationship cover them with confusion and even anxiety. Patterns which have been witnessed in childhood between Mum and Dad may surface as an unwritten rulebook, both partners carrying their own. Put all that together as a package and it doesn't take an Einstein to realize it's a problematical equation.

If you accept that it's more likely women, rather than men, will look for a solution to an emotional problem, on the grounds that women are taught to care and men to pretend nothing's the matter, then this book by Nancy Good may give you a few keys to tricky problems. We can never change anyone else. They'll only change if they want to. However, changing your reaction to someone, or trying a new, perhaps more honest, tactic can show significant results.

Sometimes you'll need to learn, acknowledge, and accept responsibility for things about yourself, and your contribution to stumbling blocks in a relationship. Often it's only possible to get that insight through the objective eyes or someone outside, perhaps a counsellor or close friend, or even your partner. This book, though, will help you think.

I think Nancy Good sums up the difficulties many women face when she writes 'When you love a difficult man, you often feel more anger than love, more disappointment than understanding, more contempt than admiration. Your love does not feel deep and infinite; in fact, it seems to have disappeared altogether.' If the saving graces of his personality and your relationship can still surface, and ease that pain, you may decide to do your best to improve the situation.

When I told a friend I was writing a foreword for a book, entitled *How to Love a Difficult Man*, he asked. 'Why would you want to?' As Nancy Good writes, 'A difficult man is any man . . .' Which brings me back to where I started—no-one is perfect, and I think both sexes could benefit from reading and thinking about Nancy Good's suggestions.

Gill Cox
Problem Page Editor, Woman's Realm

The Dilemma: Can a Woman Ever Get What She Wants from the Man in Her Life?

Never treats me sweet and gentle the way he should;
My poor heart is sentimental not made of wood
He don't love me like I love him nobody could
I got it bad and that ain't good.
—DUKE ELLINGTON
and PAUL FRANCIS WEBSTER

They ain't never gonna love you any better, babe
And they're never gonna love you right.
—JANIS JOPLIN

A DIFFICULT man is lovable but hateful, charming but rude, delicious but disgusting, stable but destructive, selfish but giving, inconsiderate but thoughtful, offensive but endearing. In other words, a giant contradiction. He makes you feel good one moment, causes you pain and anger the next. And

1

to make things worse, not only do you still love him despite everything, you want him. Or at least today you do. Tomorrow may be different. You're never sure if you want him because you love him, or because you need him, or just out of habit. But one thing is certain. He has been, and still is, a powerful influence in your life. Sometimes for better, sometimes for worse. He is your difficult man.

If you asked any group of women if they were married to or living with men who were difficult, almost all would say yes. This is partly because our society encourages men to act in ways women would never dream of. A little boy who comes home from playing with his clothes torn and filthy may be chided by his parents for sloppiness or lack of thoughtfulness, but underneath that, his parents let him know he's a real boy. Historically, girls were encouraged to act properly, to show outward consideration for others before themselves, to behave well, to keep clean, to be considerate, and keep quiet. And never to ask for things or make demands, especially not for themselves. While the last twenty years of feminism have given women a much stronger sense of their true abilities, power, and personal ambitions, centuries of cultural programming and years of family patterning remain.

In my practice as a psychotherapist, I have spoken to hundreds of women over the years—lawyers, accountants, housewives, secretaries, teachers, artists, musicians. Despite their seeming differences, many share one thing in common: they love difficult men whose behavior and its consequences make them feel frustrated, disappointed, angry, and sad. As a woman myself, I also have known the unhappiness that comes from loving a difficult man. We have all gone through our adult lives seesawing between loving a man and not loving him, until the relationship feels like torture. A woman's ambivalence and confusion about the man in her life—a husband, a lover, a companion—prevents her from feeling joyful, safe, secure, and content. Not surprisingly, you may retaliate for feeling deprived by holding back your passionate love, become suspicious or nagging, all the while waiting for him to change into someone who will reciprocate in loving you the way you love him—and more important—in the way you want to be loved. The way this difficult man is when he's with you makes you live in a romantic limbo somewhere between heaven and hell. Here are the problems you have most frequently encountered with him:

He pretends to have no feelings and makes fun of you for having so many (does not recognize your inner emotional life).

He takes his anger out on you in destructive ways.

He's either so passive or so controlling you could scream.

The passion is gone from the relationship. You might as well be his mother.

He ignores your needs in bed. The attempts he made to satisfy you when you first met have long since disappeared.

He tunes you out when you're angry. You're left feeling hopeless.

He rarely tells you he loves you or appreciates you, but wants praise from you all the time.

He flirts with other women and claims you're the crazy one for being upset.

He's generous with money, but he's rarely home.

He can't seem to hold a job, or get ahead in the one he has.

He never wants to go out—to a show or a romantic
dinner.

A difficult man may be one who is violent toward you or
others, suffers from an addiction to or abuse of drugs or alcohol, or perhaps engages in compulsive behavior, like gambling. But most often the difficult man is one who makes you
unhappy in less dramatic, more subtle ways. Perhaps he does
not give you emotional support or help with your problems
—maybe he doesn't even listen. He might be a man who
always has to be right and win, someone who not only can't
walk away from a fight but goes out of his way to pick them;
even when you offer the most practical, obvious solution, he
still won't quit. Or maybe he's just the opposite—quiet, passive, and unresponsive—so that you're the one yelling and
complaining all the time. Your difficult man might be perfectly
rational and easy to communicate with about anything but a
particular subject—money, vacations, gifts, the holidays, your
career plans, marriage. Or maybe you two don't communicate
at all.

One of the most important things to know and remember
—and one of the easiest to forget—is that men have exactly
the same needs as women. Despite their seeming arrogance
and apparent pride in misbehaving, their desire for a good
relationship and their will to work at it is probably just as
strong as yours—it's just buried under years of training that
says to be a "real man" means not to care. It is hard to believe
that he cares when he's screaming at you in a restaurant,
refusing to diaper the baby while the three-year-old is crying,
or flaunting his flirtation with another woman. You may, of
course, decide that your relationship is not worth saving. But
if you still love your difficult man and want to see things get

better instead of worse, then you will find in these chapters ways of working out the problems between you so that you can have a more satisfying life. Although your man may be as upset about the problems as you are, he is not likely to be the one to initiate improvements in a troubled situation. Though women no longer sit by the fire waiting for their men to return, they remain the spiritual keepers of the hearth, and most often are the pathfinders on the couple's trail to intimacy. And blazing new trails to a better relationship is like so many responsibilities. If you don't do it, it doesn't get done. In light of everything else women have to do these days, taking the initiative here may feel like one job too many. And perhaps it is. But if you feel deprived in your relationship because your man is difficult, chances are the situation will not improve unless you take the first steps to discover your problems, their sources, and possible solutions. To create an emotionally fulfilling life with your mate, you must first commit yourself to what I call emotional risk taking. And second, you must know the psychological score. Once you've learned to take emotional risks, you not only improve your relationship with your man, but you also enrich your relationships with others and enhance your self-confidence. And knowing the psychological score means that you'll know the underlying psychological reasons why he acts the way he does. Once you know the causes for his problems, you will no longer have to either blame yourself when he acts badly (and thus lose self-confidence), or blame him and thus push him away. First, what exactly is emotional risk taking?

Emotional Risk Taking

Ordinarily, we think of taking risks in terms of feats that require extraordinary courage or physical derring-do: Jean-Claude Killy racing down the slopes, Evel Knievel jumping over the Snake River Canyon, Sally Ride flying up into outer space. Yet emotional risk taking occurs all the time. People who take these special risks do not inspire headlines or earn medals; in most cases, their rewards are intensely personal and may never be known to anyone else but themselves. Still, their courage to take a chance—to risk change—is just as great, and their task just as dangerous.

The dictionary defines risk as "the possibility of meeting danger or suffering harm or loss." Anyone who has survived an emotional crisis will tell you that confronting emotional dangers is just as risky and frightening as facing physical ones. But the emotional skills needed to deal with it are quite different. A man with the courage to walk a high wire may not necessarily have the courage to face and meet his wife's needs for intimacy. Similarly, unless we are very, very lucky, we may not have ever learned these skills. Instead, it seems that we learn many "risk avoidance" skills—from our relationships with parents, teachers, relatives, siblings, friends, others. We are brought up to believe that many things—such as good relationships—just happen, if we're lucky. But that's almost never the case. Couples who have good relationships work at them. It takes skill, time, effort, self-awareness, and risk, but it's worth it.

Of course, taking emotional risks doesn't mean jeopardizing your well-being; if you fail, you won't break your neck or die, though as you begin taking these risks, you may feel as if you will perish in the attempt. Fear is what makes emotional risk taking so dangerous and difficult. Just the thought of experiencing fear is so terrifying a prospect for most of us that we never let the thought that we might be afraid enter our minds. Instead of letting ourselves feel and express fear, we bottle it up, hoping it will go away. But it never does, and the feelings that take its place are worse.

Many of us become fearful when we get close to someone. And when that fear becomes too strong, we cut ourselves off from the emotional and physical intimacy we all crave. Intimacy requires emotional risk taking, yet risk taking inspires fear. To succeed, then, you must face your fear.

Arlene decided to face her fear and take an emotional risk with Joe. Arlene is a saleswoman with a large computer firm; Joe is a photographer. They have dated on and off for months, making commitments to each other, only to break them. Arlene has reluctantly agreed to date Joe again, and during their first dinner together, Joe announces that he cannot be happy without her and that he wants to plan their future. He also confesses that sex will never be as good with any other woman as it was with her. After this dramatic speech Joe promises that he will call her in a day or two, and Arlene returns home cautiously optimistic. When a week passes without a call from Joe, Arlene is furious but not surprised. When she reaches Joe, he tells her that he is going on assignment in Rome but that he planned to call her when he returned. Variations on this scene have been played out several times before in Arlene and Joe's relationship, but this time Arlene is ready to take a risk. She tells Joe very firmly that he is

7

mistreating her by acting as if he wants to be close and then running away and that this behavior makes it impossible for her—or any woman—to take his feelings seriously. She adds in a sad tone of voice that she can't continue their relationship if he keeps disappearing instead of talking things out. Arlene ends by asking him point-blank, "What should I do when you disappear? Isn't it time I looked for someone else?"

Though Arlene has long understood that Joe disappears whenever he feels overwhelmed and frightened by his strong feelings for her, she also realizes that she is not happy with this situation and admits that she has lost patience with Joe's problem. Arlene's solution is extreme —you usually don't have to threaten to end a relationship to get what you want—but it provides a good example of emotional risk taking. By telling Joe exactly what he is doing and how she feels about it, Arlene has left herself open for a possible loss: Joe may reject her; there may be no more romantic evenings spent planning a future together; she may be alone. But even if Arlene does lose Joe, she will still come out ahead. Either way, Arlene will be able to begin to get what she wants—a real, reciprocal relationship—either with a changed Joe or with someone new.

Here are more examples of women taking emotional risks and getting what they want.

After getting into bed, George begins to caress Harriet. She is happy that he wants to make love—it's been a while—and she responds. Suddenly George is ready to have intercourse but Harriet is hardly ready. He has barely touched her. In the old days Harriet might have laid there silent and miserable or screamed, "You don't care about me. You never ask me what I want." Now, instead, she stops George and firmly says this is all happening too fast for her. She tells him she would like to go more slowly and she tells him exactly what she would like. "I'd love for you to stroke my back and my thigh. And I need you to touch my clitoris until I am ready to have intercourse too." George becomes silent and turns away. He says, "You're always criticizing me." Harriet tells him how much she loves him and that she loves making love to him, that he used to do these things when they first met. She thinks they have to be able to tell each other what they like in bed. She asks what he wants her to do. But George refuses to return to making love. Harriet tells him, "I'm very upset that you don't want to hear what I need. How is your turning away going to help solve our problem?" She goes to sleep restlessly. Although Harriet feels anxious, she knows that she will never get what she wants in bed if she doesn't take this risk. For three months Harriet and George repeated this scenario, but with Harriet remaining extremely loving though firm in her resolve. George eventually came to understand and to hear what she was saying without feeling too threatened to do what she asked. Their sexual life is now mutually satisfying and exciting, and much to their surprise, this new kind of communication has spilled over to the rest of their life together.

Another example:

He wants his daughter to stay with you for the whole summer (she lives with her mother), and to go on the European vacation with the two of you that has been planned. You like his daughter but know that after a week the three of you will drive each other a little crazy. His daughter will be bored silly looking at castles, and you and your husband have only this time in Europe to be together alone all year. The summer will be ruined for everyone. You take a risk and tell him that you don't like the idea. He is furious with you and thinks you're asking him to make a choice between his daughter and you. You feel threatened but stick to your feelings and tell him that he is ignoring what he knows is best for everyone in this situation. After several weeks of arguing you arrive at a plan. His daughter will stay with you for a month at the beginning of the summer and two weeks at the end. You and he will go to Europe alone together in the middle. During that time she will go on a tour with a group of children her own age. Your husband tells you that he's glad you insisted that the plans be changed. This is really better for all of you.

And one more:

You'd planned to go to the movies together but when you meet him at home he is nasty and cold. In the old days you might have tried to talk him into going and then have had an awful time because he's sulking. Instead, you take a risk and say that you'd really like to have a pleasant and relaxed evening. It might be better if you went alone if he can't change his mood. You end up going alone and enjoy the movie. When you come home, he is loving and thoughtful. He's able to tell you that he had a terrible day and needed time to himself. You tell him, "I hope the next time you can tell me what's bothering you and what you need right away."

Just as Olympic champions are rewarded only after they have worked at their sport and perfected their skill for years, you may have to take many emotional risks—always keeping your ultimate goal of a better relationship in mind—before you get what you want. Always remember, though, to invest your time and energy not just with any man, but only with a man who is very important in your life, because emotional risk taking requires concentration and effort. You'll have to be both an observer and a participant in understanding and controlling your feelings, while at the same time knowing what the possible dangers and rewards are for each risk you take. You may also have to change your own behavior for a short time to help you see more clearly what your next steps will be. Though this sounds almost impossible, especially in that most highly charged predicament called love, women have been taking emotional risks for years and ultimately getting what they want. And you can too. We will explore in these chapters what kinds of risks you can take in problem situations to improve your relationship.

The Psychology of Love

It's taken years for you and your man to become who you are as individuals. Almost from the day you were born, you watched and learned—consciously and unconsciously—how people who love each other act, how relationships work, and what kind of behavior is acceptable and what is not. Since no one's family is perfect, at times we pick up attitudes, information, and values about ourselves and our relationships in general that can hinder us in developing the kinds of emotional bonds that we need in order to grow. We carry these feelings about ourselves and others forever. Only by being aware of them can you learn to deal with them more effectively. Knowledge, of course, is power. To be psychologically strong enough to improve your relationship with a difficult man, then know the psychology of love, the psychological score, so to speak. Why does he do what he does, and why do you react the way you do? Each problem area discussed throughout this book will not only tell you what risks you must take, but what exactly is really going on between the two of you.

For example, many couples complain about the problem that Jim and Marsha have. After living together for six months, Jim resumed an old pattern of his—arriving late without calling. Marsha complained, of course, but it didn't help. Jim would keep her waiting in restaurants, outside theaters, and at home.

One of the reasons that Jim is acting this way now is something we are all subject to, namely, the placing on to significant people in the present the feelings and thoughts that we had toward significant people from our past. Psychologists call this "transference." To make this simpler, Jim, now that he has created a home with Marsha, unconsciously wants and expects his life with Marsha to be the same as his life was with his parents. Jim's father always kept his mother waiting, and as Jim got older, in order to be close to his dad, he joined his dad in this "keep mother waiting" routine. Mother was always angry, of course. Now, fifteen years later, Marsha has unknowingly fallen into the role of being just like Jim's mother—standing around tapping her foot. Unknowingly, Jim and Marsha are reliving Jim's life at home. Jim and Marsha are also in a power struggle. (Power struggles are a common trap for couples. This will be discussed in a later chapter.) Marsha should figure out what is going on psychologically. She will realize that Jim's repetition of the childhood pattern he watched his parents perform is part of the problem. Jim is making Marsha into his mother and she is willingly playing her part. Marsha must then take an emotional risk. Step one is for her to try to say nothing about Jim's lateness. She is thus doing the opposite of Jim's mother, breaking the chain of habit. She also must school herself never to make any arrangement with Jim in which she knows she could be kept waiting and will become angry. Once Marsha does these two things, she has stepped out of the mother role that Jim unconsciously assigned to her and she has dropped out of the power struggle. The waiting game between them thus ends. Jim now has the opportunity to be different from the way he acted with his mother. When Marsha changes the game, Jim is freed to take responsibility for his lateness and very likely will try harder to be on time.

Throughout the situations discussed, we will see how your background, and your difficult man's, may be contributing to the problems you have.

Are Women "Too Emotional"?

Many women think that it is a liability to be intensely emotional. Whenever anyone says, "What are you getting so upset about?" "You feel every little thing." "You're too sensitive. I never meant that. You're blowing this way out of proportion," we may resent their comments, but deep down we believe they're right. It is true that the female of the human species displays her emotional sensitivity to a much greater extent, still, than the male. But it is not necessarily true that women blow things out of proportion. In difficult moments, often they are feeling and expressing for both themselves and their mates. Women seem to resonate to the slightest emotional off-note because they have been trained—by parents, society, friends, and lovers—to do so. In 1860 author George Eliot reminded us that women have been feeling while men have been fighting since the days of Hector and Hecuba.

> . . . the women . . . watching the world's combat from afar,
> filling their long, empty days with memories and fears, outside
> the men, quenching memory in the strong light of purpose,
> losing the sense of dread . . . in the hurrying ardour of action.

One of the reasons that you are so upset with the man in your life (while he may not seem to be feeling much at all) is that you are the one who detects, absorbs, processes, and puts into words the emotional ebb and flow for the relationship for both of you. Having this vast array of feelings to draw upon is analogous to being a painter with a well-equipped studio, but you may feel compelled to use every single color, whether it really fits or not. Feelings, like art, are rarely neat, and intense feelings, especially those we hold inside over time, can be downright sloppy. Becoming skillful in any medium, be it painting or expressing and working with feelings, takes practice. As you become aware of your emotions and where they come from, you will be better equipped to survive marriage or living together.

Men are generally taught either to hide their feelings or to express them as "acceptable" emotions or through "acceptable" responses (for example, acting angry when they're really afraid, or yelling instead of crying) that seem more "masculine." How well your relationship develops may depend a lot on how well you understand him—even when he doesn't understand himself or hides how he feels. The other night I was talking to a friend who had just come from having dinner with her ex-husband for the first time since their divorce a year before. At one point they talked about their country home and how scared she used to be of the night noises, how he was always the one to go and investigate, and how he would make fun of her for being afraid. For the first time her ex admitted that he, too, was scared of those noises and what he might have found. Though my friend felt closer to him and freer to be herself because he revealed that he had shared her fear, she also felt sad because it was too late for their marriage. In a later chapter we will explore how to read the emotional "hieroglyphics" of men like her ex who disguise what they feel.

Who Is the "Perfect Couple"?

We see them everywhere—on television, in movies, magazine ads, and books. They even have names, like Ozzie and Harriet and Ron and Nancy. We have been taught that the "perfect couple" isn't an ideal or a fantasy, but a commonplace. Despite the fact that this couple doesn't exist, we still all believe that:

—the perfect couple does not have conflicts. There may be little spats about traditional issues—his leaving socks on the floor, her spending too much on a dress, both of them forgetting to call the plumber—but nothing too serious.

—the spats the perfect couple does have are brief, not probed, and soon forgotten.

—the perfect couple does not disagree or argue in front of others.

—the perfect couple fits together like hand in glove.

—the perfect couple does not question or feel confused about their personal or family goals for the future. They agree on these goals; that's why they're perfect.

—both partners in the perfect couple are clear about their roles and their partner agrees with them.

—the perfect couple is absolutely secure about its ideas on child-raising, money management, care of the house, and where to live. Any disagreements would be mild and joked about.

—the perfect couple has perfect sex.

—the perfect couple does not have deep feelings that trouble them. They *never* have big problems.

Given the total unreality of the perfect couple, it's no wonder none of us can ever measure up to this no matter how hard we try. The ideal anything isn't bad in and of itself. The real problem is that to achieve an ideal, you must adhere to certain values, many of which are unrealistic or destructive. In terms of values, the perfect-couple concept tells us that arguments are bad—in a perfect world you argue only with people you do not like—never with someone you love. Some people go so far as to believe that people who argue are "unbalanced" or misfits. Another value concerns maturity. In our society couples who know where they are going in life are mature; those who are not one hundred percent sure must be childish or lazy or stupid. And a third value concerns upbringing and correctness. It is considered a sign of a bad upbringing to argue or question the way in which you choose to lead your life. Presented this way, some of these beliefs may sound alien. Yet we all have been influenced by them at some time in our lives.

When the perfect couple breaks up, which they do as often as the rest of us mediocre types, their friends and family are as shocked as if the couple had appeared nude in *Playboy.* An indecent event has occurred. What these observers never seem to realize is that all along this couple's perfection existed only in the eyes of the beholders. The rest of us have a need to idealize these couples for a few reasons. One is that this idealizing process, or fantasizing, takes our minds off our own everyday reality of frustration and stress. We can dream of that magical trouble-free relationship and feel that their existence offers hope. Another explanation for fantasizing is that we can picture a perfect couple as the perfect parents we never had but desperately wanted. An example of how our idealization of others works occurred in a therapy group I was leading. A former beauty queen, now living in a penthouse with her apparently wealthy boyfriend, reveals how miserably inadequate she feels, how unhappy she is with her boyfriend, that, in fact, they are on the edge of bankruptcy. Across the room an average-looking single man who was sure that the beauty queen had "everything" is shocked when his fantasy about her life is shaken by the truth.

The trouble with idealizing a "perfect" anyone, especially the "perfect" couple, is that you and your mate never seem to measure up—and you never will. As a result, you dislike yourself and him whenever you argue. "How come we're not more like them. *They* never talk to each other like this," you say. But you really don't know what "they" do. In fact "they" are often living in a flimsy house of cards. One mild gust and the structure collapses. Relationships with anyone—friend, lover, or husband—that have endured conflict are stronger. (Constant conflict, of course, is something else, and as I will discuss later, is a signal that some type of counseling or therapy is needed.)

To say what you feel or not to say what you feel, that is a question. We each have strong, sometimes frightening feelings. But it is not the strong feelings we all have that damage our relationships, but *the way in which we use them.*

Redefining the "Perfect Couple"

If you compare this description of characteristics of the new, improved "perfect" couple with the one given a few pages back, you'll see they have little in common. The new perfect couple is resilient. The couple may disagree, even argue, but then can resume life together in a loving way. The new perfect couple is spontaneous. They can agree to permit room for change, changing the course of their lives, changing their opinions, changing their moods, changing decisions. The new perfect couple is able to be intimate with or without the presence of others. They are essentially supportive of each other's growth. This couple can accept and understand each other emotionally, though not to the point where differences must be hidden. The new perfect couple tries to express feelings, then lets go of these feelings without holding grudges. And the new perfect couple cares deeply about each other despite the awareness of their differences.

The underlying values are also different. First, emotional richness is treasured. Both partners desire to be fully aware of all the feelings human beings possess and to have these feelings available to them. Second, the new perfect couple knows that maturity means a deep commitment to struggle through difficulties as well as to share pleasures together. The third value is knowing that the way things look to others is less important than the way you, the couple, feel. You value your internal self and your relationship more highly than external approval. Trying to be like this new "perfect" couple is not easy either, but the rewards are worth it—even if the moments when you arrive at "perfection" are few in the beginning. Once you have a willingness to take emotional risks and to understand yourself and your man psychologically, the possibilities are unlimited.

Feeling frustrated, angry, and unhappy with the man you love is a lonely, tortured way to live. One minute you adore him, the next he's a rat; you think that your life will never be the way you want it. It's hard to feel committed to a relationship that makes you feel this way, even if you're married. Making a commitment to emotional risk taking is not easy either. But you want, and deserve, more than a relationship held together by resignation, anger, disappointment, and

19

hopelessness. When you first fell in love, life seemed exciting and full of possibilities. Imagine how wonderful it will be to wake up in the morning, look at the man you love, and feel optimistic, knowing that you can tell each other what you want and that you will each give and take happily. How do you love a difficult man? The answers are within this book. All you need is the courage.

The Man Who Fears Commitment

I wanna be loved by you,
Just you and nobody else but you
I wanna be loved by you alone,
I wanna be kissed by you . . . alone, poo-poo-pa-doop.
—H. RUBY, B. KALMAR, H. STOTHART

If evolution, as applied to sex, teaches any one lesson plainer than another, it is the lesson that the monogamic marriage is the basis of all progress.
—ANTOINETTE BROWN BLACKWELL, 1875

THE word "commitment" has several definitions, among them, "a decisive moral choice that involves a person in a definite course of action," "the act of committing to the trust," and "a state of being bound by emotional ties or intellectual conviction to a given ideal." When you are in love, the definite course of action or commitment you want to make is to him, and for him to want to do the same for you. But what given ideal or form do you want your commitment to follow? The answer is monogamy, which is defined as "being married to one person at a time," or, more usefully, "the condition of having a single mate at any one time." For our purposes, monogamy will mean "the condition of having a romantic and sexual relationship with only one person at any one time." In order to have a successful long-term intimate romantic relationship, you must both commit to monogamy. Of course, not everyone agrees with this idea. Dorothy Parker wrote:

> *Accursed from their birth they be*
> *Who seek to find monogamy,*
> *Pursuing it from bed to bed—*
> *I think they would be better dead.*

The man who fears commitment would agree with Ms. Parker. David is such a man.

Georgette met David at a seminar six months ago. They had many common interests and enjoyed going to museums and seeing plays on weekends. Though there were strong sexual vibrations between them, neither made a sexual advance for five months. For the last month, however, they have been sexually involved. They see each other several times a week, and Georgette feels that they're both very much in love. Last week Georgette mentioned that she was not seeing other men, perhaps hoping that David would agree not to see other women. She had come to care so much about him that the thought of him seeing other women hurt her. Much to her surprise, David was taken aback by her statement, and he explained that he hadn't been seeing anyone but planned to if he met someone who interested him. He hadn't thought of their relationship as a "marriage" and didn't think that kind of commitment ever worked out well. Soon after, David was too busy to see Georgette often. A few weeks later they stopped dating completely.

David fits exactly into the category of men called "the great pretenders." They love to act in an intimate and close way. They even like to "play house," as long as they don't have to make an actual commitment to the other person. It is important to understand the many underlying psychological reasons why a man is unwilling to be in an exclusive relationship so that when you are rejected in this way, you don't blame yourself for being somehow inadequate. Georgette, like many women, blamed herself in a subconscious effort to protect her own deeply rooted fantasies about men. "I should never have mentioned commitment to him," she says. But she is wrong. The subject of how committed you both are must be raised. Women who insist on maintaining these fantasies rather than finding out the truth often have a rude awakening. Yvette, for example, married a man from Brazil and went to live there before she discovered that his idea of marriage was that he would romance other women while she stayed at home. He was even surprised that this would upset her. Since they had never discussed the subject, both had assumed that the other wanted what they wanted. What Yvette got was a part-time lover, which few women are happy to settle for.

We are going to carefully examine the possible emotional reasons why any man (or woman) would flee from a relationship the way David did and then look at what you can do to change the outcome. Of the many men who fear commitment, some eventually can be helped to feel safe enough to take the plunge. But first, let's look at why Georgette felt impelled to "pop the question" about monogamy in the first place. More and more women find themselves in this very risky and until recently exclusively male position of doing the asking.

Approach-Avoidance Phenomena

There is a variation in the cha-cha called the chase, where one partner chases the other. At any moment, however, the "chaser" taps his or her partner on the shoulder, and the couple whirls around. Now their roles are reversed. This dance clearly illustrates the approach-avoidance phenomenon. In each relationship one pursues while the other is pursued. In this way, they will maintain a distance between them that they both feel is tolerable for their individual psychological survival. Since in the past decade or so, it has become socially acceptable for the woman to initiate the discussion of commitment and marriage, some men have assumed what used to be the woman's position; now he may be the one who is pursued. A comfortable distance between two people, whoever maintains it, is absolutely necessary for anyone's psychic health. This distance, of course, is constantly changing depending on the individual partner's growth. You know that plants crowded too closely compete for nutrients, water, and light, and none grow as well as they would given ample space. We humans have a similar need for space, both physical and emotional. A couple whose situation illustrates this situation is June and Stewart.

Since June and Stewart moved in together a year ago, June has been discussing marriage like a general plotting the takeover of a city. She had plans as to when this marriage should occur and the problems they needed to overcome before then. Stewart was anything but cooperative during these talks. Finally, though, he agreed to marriage and has even started looking at engagement rings. Suddenly June has had difficulty sleeping and expresses anxiety about the marriage.

Now that Stewart has stopped expressing his anxiety about the marriage, June is doing it for both of them. Although their individual reasons may vary somewhat, June and Stewart are both afraid of

1. merging with each other

2. being enveloped by the other

3. losing their autonomy, and

4. being hurt, rejected, and abandoned.

They each also fear their angry feelings toward the other, and worry about whether they each can resist the temptation of acting on sexual feelings toward other people. These are all very common fears, and I'll discuss them further in this chapter.

Here is another example of a couple doing the approach-avoidance dance. During their two years of dating, Larry told Rochelle that he did not want to date other women and wanted her to live with him. From writing her poems to sending her flowers, he acted like a man smitten by love. Rochelle hesitated, having only recently ended her marriage, but Larry persisted and she finally suggested they take an apartment together. Suddenly, Larry's attitude changed. He became more flirtatious with other women and dragged his feet when it came to looking for an apartment.

Although Rochelle and Larry eventually did move in together, their relationship endured many difficult periods. Much of the arguing resulted because Rochelle wanted closeness, which Larry was now rejecting emotionally, though he was staying in the relationship. Many arguments that couples have about very specific issues can be seen in terms of approach-avoidance phenomena. Traditionally, men are concerned about maintaining enough distance, while women are concerned with maintaining closeness. It sometimes seems that we've been raised to work at cross purposes. The man who maintains a distance from you is not "more mature" or "healthier" than you are because he *appears* to need you less. He can seem to be composed because you are making him feel wanted. Don't criticize yourself because, right now, you are brave enough to discuss monogamy while he does the other half of the approach-avoidance dance. Since so many men do fear commitment, chances are that you will be the one raising the issue of commitment. You will be better prepared for the task if you are completely aware of all the reasons that he may be afraid of monogamy.

Fears of Monogamy

This hit song by Carly Simon and Jacob Brackman describes beautifully what some of his primary fears of commitment are all about.

You say that we can keep our love alive;
babe, all I know is what I see.
The couples cling and claw and drown in love's
debris.
You say we'll soar like two birds through the
clouds,
but soon you'll cage me on your shelf.
I'll never learn to be just me first, by myself.
But you say it's time we moved in together;
raised a family of our own, you and me.
Well, that's the way I've always heard it should
be,
you want to marry me; we'll marry.

Many couples' most terrible fear is that their relationship will be ruined once they start living together. One man that I know insists that the fantasy of marriage is far superior to the reality that he saw of his parents' life together. Why, he asks, should he risk any further closeness? He fears that if he and his girlfriend live together, they will make each other miserable and eventually break up anyway. The woman in his life has not run from "going steady," but she and he are both running from living together. Often a child of an unhappy marriage or whose parents separated, grows up fearing togetherness. Many people erroneously believe that they inherit the inability to have a good relationship just as they inherited Mother's red hair or Father's chin. But the truth is that even if you have learned your parents' behavior patterns, these can be changed over time if you are determined to have what your parents didn't.

Our society places a high value on being autonomous and independent. At the same time, though, we all learn to be

27

dependent on someone else. And so another fear of commitment is a fear of losing control of one's life to one's mate. We
look to our lovers for love, approval, physical warmth, financial support, and everything that goes into creating a sense of
security and well-being. If as a child you had love taken away
as punishment, you know what it's like to be controlled by
another person's disapproval. You might grow up unable to
decide what it is that makes *you* happy because you're always
wondering if it will make your spouse (or parent) happy too.
If your man is shying away from making a commitment to you,
he may be afraid because he already feels dependent on you
and imagines that you will try to control him.

When Sheila, a dance teacher, spoke to George about not
dating others and eventually living together, he reacted as if
she had just mugged him. He insisted that Sheila would try to
tell him how to spend his money and that he was sure he would
resent her for it. Sheila reassured him that she wanted their
finances to remain separate and that she would even sign an
agreement to that effect if they got married. George was relieved to hear this and, because he felt safer, he could admit
to himself and to Sheila that he wanted someday to "give her
everything she wanted." Remember, then, that the fear of
losing control of one's self and thus one's life may be frightening him even when he does love you.

Dr. Willard Gaylin, in his book *Feelings,* writes: "Feelings
are internal directives essential for human life." But the man
in your life may be afraid of his feelings, especially his negative
feelings toward you. He may reject your proposal for commitment because, unconsciously, he thinks you'll reject him once
you see his anger. One man confessed to me that he broke off
relationships before they went on too long because he didn't
want the woman to see what he was really like. Convinced that

his anger, impatience, and anxiety would turn a woman off, he broke off with each new woman after only a few months. Because his mother had given him the silent treatment whenever he got upset, he was sure other women would do the same, and he couldn't bear the rejection of that experience. How to create an environment where all your feelings, and his, can be expressed and accepted, will be explored in other chapters. However, you can let him know from the beginning that you want a relationship where all feelings are acceptable.

A Sense of Entitlement

The difference between the "haves" and the "have-nots," other than the luck of being born a Rockefeller, has a lot to do with a sense of entitlement. Whether or not the man in your life feels that he *deserves* to have all that he wants in life affects whether he'll actually get those things, whether that "thing" is a Mercedes, a country home, or a long-term relationship with you. When a man runs from a relationship, or is painfully ambivalent about it, frequently the underlying reason is that he does not feel entitled. The man in your life is not consciously aware that he doesn't think he deserves you. This feeling of being undeserving often starts in childhood when parents flaunt the special bond that they have with each other and the child feels harshly excluded. The considerate parent lets his child know that he is loved and that, when he grows up, he, too, will marry and have someone of his own. When five-year-olds go steady, they are imitating their parents and finding a way to cope with being excluded. But not all parents are happy to see their child tie the knot, since this means their tie to him will be loosened. Tears at weddings are shed as much from the pain of letting go as from joy.

Jacob, a dynamic store owner, lived for several years with Suzanne, a computer expert of a different religion. His parents' strong disapproval of Suzanne drove Jacob to break up with her. He continued to believe that his parents rejected Suzanne because of her religion until later when they rejected another woman he wanted to marry who was of the same religion. To his surprise, his parents were as unfriendly to and as critical of her as they had been of Suzanne. They did not want him to leave them psychologically for anyone else, and so they would not like any woman Jacob wed. This tug-of-war between Jacob and his parents had been going on since he was old enough to have friends. No wonder he felt guilty every time he grew close to a woman.

Another example of not feeling that you are entitled to a relationship is this situation with Jack and Alice, who have been dating for a year. Together they visit Jack's parents once a month. Jack's mother seems to be living for the day that Jack will finally get married and so she always acts anxious and happy when she asks Alice for the latest update. After every visit to Jack's parents, he and Alice argue and seem on the verge of breaking up. Alice has learned to keep quiet on the subject of marriage when Jack's parents are around; she sees that Jack's mother is doing more harm than good.

In fact, Jack does not feel entitled to have a marriage half as good as his parents have, even though his mother appears to be waiting breathlessly for an announcement. Similarly, he has trouble making enough money (as an editor of trade magazines), since he doesn't feel entitled to "the good life" either. His parents have always made him the focus of their concerns, from doing his laundry to organizing his finances, and marriage would seriously disrupt this arrangement. What Jack does feel entitled to is remaining a part of his parents' life, and not having a full life of his own. Jack also has difficulty establishing who he really is with his parents. When his mother talks about marriage with Alice, he feels that she's even choosing a wife for him. He strives for some control by staying unmarried, but in the end, he also defeats himself. Another way parents can deter a child from a relationship is to monopolize the child's attention. Victor's mother gets sick any time he plans a weekend away with a woman, and his guilt and concern about his mother's health stops him from making commitments to anyone else.

One last fear of commitment comes from the fear of sexual feelings. Lois Gould wrote in her 1970 novel *Such Good Friends*, "Hogamous, higamous, men are polygamous. Higamous, hogamous, women monogamous." Although this silly rhyme is no longer true in the extreme, men still worry more than women do that they will not be able to control their feelings of lust for other women once they've said "I'm yours." Bringing a third party into you and your partner's sex life is one of the easiest ways to avoid being intimate. Men who do this have a very high level of anxiety about closeness and they relieve it though extracurricular sexual activity.

Rather than being discouraged by what seems like an infinite number of reasons why you and he are afraid to get together, realize that it is always to your advantage to "know thy enemy." Helping the man in your life, and yourself, to be *aware* of these fears of monogamy can lead you to the one-to-one commitment that you need to begin a relationship that will give you everything you want. Being consciously aware of what scares him is your first step in gaining some control over his fear. One approach is to discuss these fears openly with him and admit that you have those fears too. You might say, for example, "I think you are scared of being controlled by me if we get married and I'm worried that you'll do the same to me. What can I say that will reassure you?"

Trusting Him: Should You or Shouldn't You?

You, of course, hope that once you have agreed to be romantically and sexually faithful to each other, you can trust him to stick to his word. As Mary Frances Butts, a poet of the 1800s has written, you hope that you can:

> *Build a little fence of trust*
> *Around today;*
> *Fill the space with loving work,*
> *And therein stay.*

. . . rather than to do what Emily Dickinson recommended when she wrote in 1862, "Trust in the unexpected." But following Ms. Dickinson's advice could help you be prepared for a sexual betrayal.

Six months ago Donna and Sam promised not to date others, though they maintained separate apartments. When Donna tried to reach Sam one Friday night, he was not home. The next morning when he came over to see her, Sam at first made excuses and then spilled the beans about the night before—a woman he worked with had been flirting with him for months, and he "gave in." Sam actually cried when he said how sorry he was and that this woman really meant nothing to him. But Donna was shaken, and very hurt and angry. She was terribly confused about whether or not to continue the relationship and wondered how she could ever trust Sam again.

After Donna recovered from the anger and hurt, her primary problem was deciding whether to continue seeing Sam. She still loves him but feels that Sam could do this to her again. Donna's situation is not unusual. According to research cited in the book *American Couples*, eleven to nineteen percent of married men have had brief affairs. The longer the men were married, the greater the percentage who'd had affairs. Men who lived with women fared worse: between nineteen and forty percent of them had had brief affairs, and again the number increased the longer the couples were together. Although the study found the numbers overall to be decreasing with more conservative attitudes, there's still the possibility that the trust between a couple will be tested at any time. Despite this, when you take a strong stand for faithfulness, you are not making a futile gesture. In some relationships, monogamy must be fought for and won over time, just like other conditions for intimacy that you may want. In one instance, unfaithfulness led to breaking up temporarily, but the relationship did not end.

Charles is a trumpet player who often works late. He and Jane, a graphics artist, dated seriously for eight months. After Jane's friend told her that Charles had had several brief affairs, Jane and Charles had a serious fight.

Jane felt humiliated and said she could not hold her head up if she continued to see Charles, so she began dating other men. During the six months they were apart, Jane missed Charles and found other men disappointing; Charles continued trying to reconcile. After discussing the problem several times, Charles revealed that he had a double standard, which he had learned from his father: A man could have other women but a woman had to be faithful to one man. Jane insisted that this was not for her, though she loved him. Finally Charles understood that Jane meant business. They got back together and began to look for an apartment together.

For there to be trust between a man and a woman, several requirements must be met. These differ from couple to couple, but one thing, however, seems clear: Most of us want to trust that our mate will not hurt us emotionally, will understand who we are, and most of all, will be there to give us what we need, both emotionally and physically. Of course, no one ever completely lives up to all of these expectations, so if you trust another person blindly, you will certainly be disappointed. For this reason it is more beneficial to you and your relationship to use these conditions for intimacy as guidelines or goals, and to always remember that monogamy has little chance unless you both make an effort to communicate directly and openly. This means voicing your suspicions, reaffirming monogamy, and getting him to do the same. The vital importance of expressing your feelings of jealousy will be discussed in a later chapter.

Most women I have spoken with desire to begin a love affair and marriage as naively trusting as they were when they were infants. They each hope that their man will be as responsive as their mothers were to their nonverbal requests for attention. Not only is this impossible, but blindly trusting *any* person one hundred percent is dangerous. You must establish the ground rules that you need to build a relationship, and like any alliance, your loyalty is created over time and tested by difficult encounters. One false move does not always mean that he will stray again, as we saw with Jane and Charles. What it does mean, though, is that something is wrong and you might even seek counseling. Monogamy is the only foundation upon which you can build the kind of real intimacy and closeness that you crave. Sexual encounters outside the relationship will weaken it and distract from the main event—the two of you. Sexual unfaithfulness is a kind of defense mechanism known as "acting out."

Men Who Are "Trouble": Diversionary Tactics

Not only do "actions speak louder than words," but sometimes people speak to us through their actions instead of words. "Men who are trouble" communicate to you through their actions in what is known as acting out. Acting out is one of many defense mechanisms. Sublimation, repression, suppression, projection—these are words that have become part of our everyday speech, and all are different methods of psychological self-defense. Defense mechanisms protect us from those menacing invaders, the feelings and thoughts that reside in our unconscious minds. When these thoughts and feelings escape from the unconscious, the conscious mind alerts a defense mechanism to fend off the invader. We each have our own invaders and our own set of defense mechanisms, almost

35

all of which were developed without our knowing participation. Yet they all specifically help us fit in within the family and social environment in which we were raised. When *Gone with the Wind*'s tempestuous heroine, Scarlett O'Hara, is left by her husband, Rhett Butler, for what may be the last time, she characteristically says, "I won't think about this today. I'll think about it tomorrow. After all, tomorrow is another day." She is using suppression to put off dealing with her feelings. She's been abandoned, a thought that she is unable to cope with then. Throughout her life Scarlett has survived by using suppression and it seems to have worked for her. Suppression has probably helped you to postpone experiencing difficult feelings, perhaps indefinitely. One of the ways the Kennedy family has contended with their personal tragedies is by involving themselves in politics and philanthropic works. They have sublimated, or channeled, their painful feelings into other areas, where they might feel hopeful in the face of hopelessness. Sublimation is an especially productive defense mechanism.

Acting out, however, is not a socially constructive defense mechanism, though it does help the individual temporarily get rid of troublesome feelings. It is an action an individual takes unconsciously to avoid having and expressing strong feelings that he fears will overwhelm him and his sense of security. Strangely enough, though, the person doing the acting out at the same time hopes, also unconsciously, that a particular person will be able to understand their inner feelings by watching their outward behavior. Someone attempting suicide in front of others—say a person who perches on a window ledge and threatens to jump—is an extreme example of this. Being chronically late for appointments is a less extreme variation on acting out. Having trouble holding a job and having affairs are still other forms of acting out.

Acting-out behavior makes it impossible to learn how to communicate better because the actions "drown out" the words. Understanding what lies behind the actions will help you in dealing with the man in your life who expresses his problems this way. The abuse of alcohol, the use of drugs, chronic financial problems, sexual infidelity, and even violence are the most virulent destructive forms of acting out. Men who act out feel everything but deny this acute sensitivity. They are so overwhelmed by their emotions that they jump into action. Women are attracted to this sensitivity and passion but can easily lose themselves in the complex problems such a man presents. The typical TV tough guy cuts a romantic figure and women stay involved with him hoping that things will get better but never understanding why they don't, or why they themselves don't leave. Gail's situation is a good example of this.

Gail and Alex met at the bank where they both worked. Alex, as a vice-president, was in a higher position than Gail and had been there longer, and so he became her mentor. She admired him and they began to date, but she could see problems ahead. Alex and his wife had been separated three years but he still spent holidays with her and his son. Six months later he left the bank for a position with a large corporation but was soon fired. He began a job search that, although he was very bright and capable, did not yield him the position he thought he deserved. Gail would complain that he seemed to be sabotaging his career, and he would promise that things would be better. Meanwhile, Alex began gambling at the racetrack the little money he had and was soon asking Gail for money. He got a job—and was fired again. Their relationship had been going on for three years and getting worse by the day. Alex still spent hours on the phone with his ex-wife, which also upset Gail. She felt trapped and despairing.

While Gail consciously wants life with a man who will better himself, she stays with Alex, who makes things worse for several reasons. Some of her reasons may be the same as yours.

1. She is afraid that she will not meet anyone else and she is terrified of being alone.

2. She thinks she may not meet anyone who will give her what she wants (security and stability), because she thinks perhaps there is something wrong with her.

3. She has loving feelings for Alex; she loves his wit, and enjoys their sexual life.

4. Gail is used to believing in promises that never pan out because her father often promised that they would someday be rich—yet they never were.

Gail eventually gained self-confidence and attempted to save the relationship. She set limits, told Alex that he could not borrow money from her and that she would not see him if he didn't get a job. She refused to see him altogether on those nights when he went to the racetrack. For a while it looked as if Alex would change for Gail, but within a few months he was gambling more and borrowing money from friends. Six months later Gail painfully accepted that Alex would not become the kind of man she wanted, and they broke up. But Gail had learned a lot about herself during these four years. Alex's severe difficulties in being independent and taking care of himself were really her problems too. When he worked at the bank, she had hoped that he would take care of her financially. Now that it was up to her, she became more serious about getting promoted. Men and women tend to pick partners whose unconscious psychological makeup is similar to their own. One partner may even act out the problems for both. You may be staying with a man who acts out, as Alex did, because he is expressing some of your own conflicts, although you will not consciously know this. Regardless of the reasons, though, for you both to have the kind of emotionally loving relationship that will help you grow, the acting out must stop. Since Gail did not want to support Alex financially, especially when he was gambling, she took a risk and tried to get him to take care of himself by saying no and telling him what he could do to save the relationship. He chose not to. Sometimes, risk taking results in losing your lover. In Phil and Sheila's case, however, it paid off.

Phil "fell in love" with Sheila when he met her at a party. He pursued her with flowers, nights on the town, and constant attention. Sheila liked Phil and loved the attention he paid her, but she smelled trouble. Phil's last girlfriend had left him in part because of his excessive drinking, and he was still hitting the bottle often. Despite this he was a successful lawyer and money was never a problem, so she continued to see Phil. There were only a few times when his drinking really came between them, but she thought it best to date other men too. She told Phil that she could never consider a serious commitment with him as long as he drank. Their relationship continued this way for two years, Sheila keeping Phil at a distance, but Phil insisting that he wanted more. Finally Phil developed stomach problems from his drinking and he decided to stop. A year later Sheila and Phil married.

Loving a man who has an addiction problem, whether it's to alcohol, drugs, or gambling, is like being in love with a married man—something always comes between you. But men with acting-out problems are often emotionally sensitive and intuitive and sometimes talented as well—all highly attractive features. Rather than break off a relationship, you may want to let him know, as Sheila did, what the ground rules must be, and, over time, evaluate if he can change, and if you can get what you want. If, however, you are living with or married to a man who has any of these problems, you may want to get some professional help to assist you to do what Alcoholics Anonymous recommends: "Detach from his problems with love." Once you actually live in the same household, your urge and need to "change" the other person can be overwhelming. It can help, also, to examine your own family history to find out where the roots of your attraction to each other began. That is what Barbara did.

Once an actress, Barbara still has a flair for the dramatic even though now she is a broker on Wall Street. For two years she and Charlie dated exclusively but they argued whenever Charlie occasionally drank too much and "got mean," as Barbara put it. Once or twice he hit her when she tried to stop him from walking out during an argument. They stopped seeing each other after one of these fights. Barbara now realizes that she is attracted to "wild" guys and that their wildness is often augmented by alcohol or drugs. Analyzing her past, she sees that the negative attention her "bad-girl" behavior got her as a teen was the only attention her parents had to offer. She distracted them from their own problems, which included her father's late nights out and his abuse of prescribed pain-killers. Now she seems to need these men who are like her father and who are "bad boys" the way she used to be a "bad girl."

We bring with us into adulthood a longing for our childhood. Relentlessly we pursue people who remind us of our parents or who create the same type of chemistry, for better or worse. Having been very close to her father, who was often high on medication, Barbara is comfortable with men "medicated" on liquor or drugs. Underneath Barbara's self-confident facade is a woman who believes her parents' judgment that she is "no good" and that no one will ever want her. Not surprisingly, she is drawn to finding men who reject her or who are trouble. As Barbara admitted how scared she was of intimacy without the protection of acting out, she became more careful and is slowly weaning herself away from men who act out. She now knows how scared she is of making a commitment to someone who will always be there for her.

Why Doesn't He Just Say "No"? The Underlying Reasons for Destroying a Commitment by Acting Out

All too rarely will a man come right out and tell the woman he's been seeing that he wants to end the relationship. She may not like what she's heard but at least she's heard it. More often, however, a change in a relationship is communicated, not verbally, but through a change in behavior. The following painful passage from Dorothy Parker's "A Telephone Call" describes one woman's reaction to such a behavior change—when he hasn't called.

> Please, God, let him telephone me now. Dear God, let him call me now. I won't ask anything else of You, truly I won't. It isn't very much to ask. It would be so little to You, God, such a little, little thing. Only let him telephone now. Please, God. Please, please, please. If I didn't think about it, maybe the telephone might ring. Sometimes it does that if I could think of something else. . . . This is the last time I'll look at the clock. I will not look at it again.

Suddenly stranded in an emotional desert after months (or years) of lush passion, this woman has returned to feeling as helpless as if she were a lost child. I hope your reaction to this situation would be outrage at this shoddy treatment rather than feeling as if you cannot survive without the man in question. But regardless of your reaction, the silent phone conveys a message that always should be delivered in person: This relationship is over. There are many other acting-out behaviors that deliver the same message: He can't see you because he works all the time or is away on vacation or business; he lets you find out through friends that he's seeing someone else; he's too strapped for cash to go anywhere with you; he uses drugs or abuses alcohol to such an extent that you cannot be with him. If you have been with a man who has told you "no" without actually telling you, then you've been shadow-boxing; you feel like fighting but there is no one there to fight with. Often when the real target of a woman's anger is unavailable, she will end up fighting herself instead, as did the woman waiting for the phone to ring.

When your man has promised to be faithful to you, and *then* suddenly acts in strange and inappropriate ways, you may feel "seduced and abandoned." Your emotions are being manipulated; you feel like he holds the strings. To add to the confusion, when you ask this man whether or not he wants the relationship to continue, he will almost always say, "Yes, of course." What makes you feel like you are "going crazy" is the double, contradictory message. When Groucho Marx invites Harpo to sit down and then pulls the chair out from under him, he's sending a double message. Or when a friend insists that you must borrow her dress (which happens to look well on you) to wear to your cousin's wedding, then worries aloud that the dress might be ruined and reminds you that it *is* her favorite dress. When you tell her that you'd rather not use it, she is outraged. You are in a "no-win" situation; you will not win favor with your friend no matter what you do.

Tammy met a Mr. Double Message-Giver at a ski house. Finding humor in the same things while also sharing a love for skiing, Tammy and Mike seemed fated to fall in love. Their relationship was intense right from the start. They saw each other five nights a week and after two months had met each other's families. One Sunday evening after a particularly nice weekend, Mike seemed cold and withdrawn, yet when Tammy tried to get him to talk, he denied there was anything troubling him. He claimed he was too busy at work that week to make plans. After the same thing happened the next weekend, Tammy confronted him. Mike said he cared about her as much as ever but thought perhaps they should date others as well. This struck Tammy as a contradiction—he wanted her but he didn't. He said he did not want to give her up, but his actions, which seemed to say the opposite, forced her to make a decision.

A man like Mike, who sends out two conflicting signals, confuses and angers the woman he loves. The problem is that he is unaware that *he* has any angry or other negative feelings toward women. He feels that he likes women and that he likes you, when, in fact, he is as terrified of saying yes to your relationship as he is of saying no. A man like Mike may have grown up in a family where his mother rarely took a stand on anything with him, so he does not expect that you will now either. He thinks that the failure of any relationship was "his fault" because he didn't want what the woman wanted—commitment. He denies to himself that he has ever been rejected by a woman; in his mind, he rejected her. On a superficial level Mike feels confident that he is attractive to women. What will help you to communicate with a double-message giver is to know that in his unconscious mind and deepest feelings he really has no confidence at all about being able to be truly close to a woman. Tammy found a way to determine what Mike really wanted. She told him that he would miss out by dating others because it would sabotage their relationship, which could never grow to be more intimate than it was. She explained to him that he was only running from his feelings toward her—both positive and negative—by dating others, and that she felt confident that they could talk things out. She went on to say that she didn't want to stagnate emotionally in this kind of relationship, even if that is what he wanted to do, and that *she* was rejecting what he offered. It was difficult, and Tammy had to say these things several times over a period of time. But she noticed that the stronger she felt about what would work for them, the less Mike felt convinced about his point of view. She still was frustrated because he had not told her what she really wanted to hear. She was about to leave him when he said he would try it her way, though he admitted that he didn't like the idea.

Several factors influence whether or not the man in your life will agree to monogamy. One is how many failed relationships he has had. Statistics show that second marriages have a higher success rate than first ones, partially because the individuals are determined to make *this* one work. Mike, like each of us, may learn from his experience that there is some validity and truth in what you and other women have said to him. Maybe he is afraid that he may never have a relationship like "other people" have, or perhaps he may have tired of the dating game. No matter what other factors are influencing him, *you* can have an effect also if:

1. You are convinced that monogamy is the only means of achieving the kind of intimacy that will ultimately give you what you want.

2. You are confident that if it does not happen with him, it will happen with someone else, and that the man you are involved with now is not the last man on earth.

3. You believe that you will be a valuable person to a man as a friend, companion, lover, or wife.

4. You feel strongly that he is a valuable person to you and that you want to be with him if he makes a commitment.

You must be sure of the above points, because if you aren't, you might be talked out of what you *know* is true. A man who wants to be with you but does not want to make a commitment to you is scared. And people who are scared will do and say desperate things to try to avoid the situation or the person that scares them. This is especially true of people who deny their fears. Instead of telling you that he is scared, your man will tell you that:

1. He's perfectly happy the way things are—why are you rocking the boat?

2. Commitments (marriages) never last—just look around you.

3. The relationship will be more exciting if you see others (or drink or take drugs).

4. He's never made a commitment before that worked, why should it with you?

5. He's not sure that you're right for him.

Though he may sound as sure of himself as Muhammed Ali before a fight, don't be swayed by a desperate man, and don't believe that what he says about you is true. If you weren't right for him, why is he still around?

A Life of Crises: When Couples Act Out Together

Many of us go through life literally "looking for trouble." Perhaps you or one of your friends is "always in a crisis," always on the verge of losing her apartment, her job, being hospitalized for one illness or another, or is in a desperate financial condition. No one escapes misfortune; bad things happen to everyone at one time or another. But the chronically besieged individual is unconsciously creating her own tragic opera. When you are preoccupied by crises, you are not free to expand yourself or your relationships. Someone who deliberately buys a dilapidated house that they cannot afford to fix will forever be shoring up crumbling walls and never get to enjoy their yard or meet their neighbors. But then, they don't really want to. Underlying all the feverish activity of crisis makers is a fear of "having more." For some people, having it all provokes more anxiety than having nothing at all. So if you and the man in your life seem engulfed by his or your recurring crises, or mutual ones, you both are addicted to these distractions from the good life. The underlying psychological reasons for this vary from person to person. The example of Deidre and Louis will illustrate what these might be.

Living in six houses in six years has not been easy for Deidre and Louis, and the arrival of their first child last year made their gypsy life-style almost untenable for her. When they married five years earlier, their goal had been to buy a house, but so far neither of them has earned enough money to make that dream come true. Each house or apartment they rented had a built-in drawback —either the owners were returning to take possession in a short time, or she and Louis found fault with the location. Louis is a skilled plumber who works for himself because he refuses to work for anyone else. But this situation does not work either because Louis manages his business so poorly. He underestimates how long a job will take and so his earnings are never sufficient. Deidre's interest in sculpting has not developed into a money-making endeavor. The odd jobs she took paid for some household expenses. Squeaking by on too little for too long has created frustration for both of them. Each one looked to the other to lead the way out.

Deidre must propose to change their unconscious marriage contract from "live and grow old and poor together" to "live and grow old and prosper together." Sporadic complaints and occasional blowups, which only scare them both, alleviate the pressure temporarily but do nothing to improve the situation that, unconsciously, neither of them wants to change. Several factors are at work here. First, Deidre's parents pampered her by giving her material things. In return, they demanded that she have no angry feelings toward them. Deidre's mother's greatest wish was that her daughter marry a wealthy man, largely because she always "had to work" to supplement Deidre's father's small income. Deidre always felt pushed by her mother, so in her mind, now that she's doing the opposite of what her parents wish, she's "in control" of her life. But in fact, Deidre is so frustrated by her borderline life-style that she would get a "real" job or go back to school if only Louis wasn't so resistant to the idea. He becomes incensed when Deidre suggests changes that would help them, so she withdraws out of fear—not that Louis will leave, but that he will be angry with her. Some facts about Louis's family also come into play. He is controlled psychologically by a very competitive father, who did moderately well in his own business. Demanding of Louis yet critical at the same time, his father takes satisfaction in bailing his son and Deidre out of their financial crises. When this happens, Louis is apologetic and grateful, and his father feels needed.

Deidre and Louis must decide to leave the psychological confines of their families if they are to succeed as a family on their own. Deidre's best bet is to start on her career despite Louis's anger, which is really only his fear that she will leave him behind. She should tell him, "I care about you and our life together and I know that we are both scared of any changes, but I am not going to leave you if I become more successful. I want us to have a better life together." If Deidre refrains from pressuring Louis right away, he will probably soon follow her example. And he might also see that even though Deidre is making changes, their relationship is still intact.

Later on, when Deidre feels capable of being on her own and if Louis does not pull his weight, she might threaten to end the relationship if Louis does not change. But this kind of ultimatum can be issued only if you sincerely feel that you cannot continue in the present circumstances and—most important—are fully prepared to follow through with it. There are numerous variations that stop short of threatening to leave and still convey how serious you are, such as, "When you act this way, it makes me want to leave you." Or "Why should I want to have a relationship with someone who doesn't care about bettering our life together?" When the woman in a relationship where there are long-term acting-out problems feels confident that she is ready for true emotional intimacy without these problems, and firmly tells her partner what she wants from him, he will often hear her as if for the first time, and respond. Make sure you know why you are "putting up with" his acting out or why you are acting out, too, before you decide on a future course.

When you have made an exclusive commitment to each other and eliminated the acting-out behaviors that were destructive to you both, you have taken the first very difficult and risky steps down the long but fascinating road toward the relationship that you want. There may be stops and detours along the way—don't cancel the trip because of them.

CHAPTER
3

Your Feelings Do Count: The Man
Who Hurts You with His Anger

The great storm raged and the power kept growin';
Dragons rose from the land below
And even now I wonder where I'm goin'
Ever since a long time ago
I've tried to let my feelin's show.

Feeling, in the broad sense of whatever is felt in any way,
as sensory stimulus or inward tension, pain or intent, is the mark of
mentality.
—SUSANNE K. LANGER, "MIND: AN ESSAY
ON HUMAN FEELING"

DIFFICULT men cause you emotional pain because they
misuse or mishandle their angry feelings. Every time he disagrees with you, dislikes what you say, or is just in a bad mood,
his anger seems to come at you like a brick. One of your
biggest jobs is to teach him how to express his anger and

differences of opinion directly, clearly, and honestly without insulting, criticizing, or intimidating you. When you live with a man who hurts you with his anger, you must let him know how his communication affects you and what your limits are. Here is an example of a typical situation.

Tony is a wonderful guy most of the time—except when he loses his temper, which can happen suddenly and without warning. He and his wife, Maria, are both gregarious and can talk a blue streak. At a party the other night Maria had the floor. She was telling the story of the time they ran out of gas and got a lift from a truck driver who turned out to be a country and western singer and entertained them all the way to the gas station at the next exit on the Massachusetts Turnpike. At this point in her story, Tony interrupted her and in a harsh tone of voice said, "You don't know what you're talking about. That was in Connecticut. You're messing up the story." Maria was mortified and the group fell silent. She wanted only to get past this awful moment, so she said, "Well, then, you tell the story." She was quiet for the rest of the evening. She never mentioned the incident when they got home, because she knew it would start a fight.

Here is another situation in which the woman is emotionally hurt by her man's inappropriate, misdirected expression of his angry feelings. Connie had started working as a film editor eight months ago after leaving graduate school. It had been a rough time for her, since she was learning everything new. She and William had been living together for three years. Though he was involved in several small businesses, he never seemed to worry about work the way Connie did. William's responses to Connie's feelings were erratic; nonetheless, she decided to tell him how awful work had been this particular day and how sure she was that she'd be fired. When she did, William exploded, "You think you're the only one with problems. You make a big deal out of everything, and I'm tired of hearing about it. Why don't you stop complaining for a change!" Connie was devastated and felt like a fool.

Tony and William both suffer from what I call occasional "attacks" of explosive or just hurtful anger, that are very separate from their otherwise pleasant personalities. Though these attacks are not caused by the woman, she is the object, since she's the closest and most trusted person in the man's life. The real cause for this momentary intense anger is unclear but can be discovered. William and Tony feel similarly anxious and inadequate but hide behind a wall of rage. Tony worries a lot whether people really like him and Maria, because he sees himself and Maria as one person. At the same time he is also jealous of the attention Maria gets. William's explosion is the product of his unexpressed anxieties about his own work. He does not allow himself to feel insecure, but when Connie verbalizes her fears, he can barely contain himself. William is a Mr. Fix-It. If he can't fix something, like Connie's insecurity, he feels desperate.

You can better grasp the real reason for his explosion if you remember that you are a convenient and trusted target—not the cause—of it. But much more important for your relationship is that you state how you feel and how you wish to be treated. You will fight back by telling him each time—and every time—that you don't like what he says to you and that you are upset (or angry or disappointed). Next, go on to explain another way that he might have responded that would make you feel closer to him. Your man will also learn by following your example, so keep your tone, your words, and your message consistent with the way you'd like him to respond to you. Loud criticisms and verbal attacks make most women feel either wounded or provoke them into a counter-attack. Neither response satisfies. This next section will show you how to protect yourself, so that a constructive expression of the differences and feelings between you can follow.

Breaking Habits: Teaching Him (and Yourself) Feeling Responses

Learning new ways to respond to old feelings and situations is not easy. Any longtime habit—be it nail-biting, smoking, or your backhand in tennis—is an automatic response to a stimulus. We do it without thinking. When you decide to break a habit, you must be acutely aware of your actions and think at times when you normally wouldn't. This is an effort for most of us.

During Connie and William's argument about work, she blames herself when he criticizes her. Connie's habitual response to criticism is to be speechless and feel like a fool. William's fault finding is also habit. Thus the two of them are caught up in destructive habits that keep them apart. If Connie wants to correct this, she must change her response first. She can wait and hope that one day William will magically be different, without her instruction, but it will never happen. If things continue in this direction, she'll end up nursing her resentment and anger until her love for him dies.

Two people in love tend to see each other as objects from their past anyway, since love arouses (unconsciously) all of our infant and childhood loving experiences. To break out of old emotional patterns, you may first have to drop an "emotional bomb." The shock or intensity of it might jolt the other person enough that you will be able to clear away the clouds of past experiences that hide and distort your understanding of the present. It may also help to get him to see and respond to you differently from the way he has to the love objects from his past. There are several ways for Connie to drop a bomb: She can say something different from what she usually does and react in a way that lets William know that she wants their relationship to accommodate all her feelings and be a place where he can express himself directly without verbally berating her. Many of those small bombs may have to be dropped before you've made way for a new form of communication.

First, she has to inform him that when he says, "You make a big deal out of everything, why don't you stop complaining for a change," he is criticizing her in a destructive, attacking manner that she does not like. She may add that she does not like *him* very much then either. She can suggest several alternative responses that William might try instead.

1. "I don't like that you become nasty with me when you are anxious. I would much rather hear about your anxious feelings directly." (This response explains to him that his anger comes from anxiety in this case.)

2. "I can understand if you don't feel like hearing about my work problems tonight, but why can't you just tell me that you're tired and don't feel like listening to me tonight instead of trying to wipe me out entirely." (This response deals with the surface dynamics alone and may

5 5

threaten him less. He might be able to admit to being tired, though he would not agree that he is anxious.)

3. "I know that when I talk about my insecurity it makes you upset because you don't know what to say. What I need from you is to hear that you think I'm good at my job and they'd be nuts to fire me." (Connie tells William how to talk to her. This shows him a better way to respond and also gets her what she needs—his support.)

Suggestions like these provide you and your man ways to improve your relationship instead of stagnating or ending it out of frustration, anger, and what seem to be insurmountable misunderstandings. However, do not expect that he will voluntarily repeat your words at the beginning and especially not in the heat of anger.

Communication improves as a result of the cumulative effort, keeping at these suggested responses relentlessly, for months perhaps, until you both are convinced that you are truly serious. If you communicate contempt, rage, or impatience, you cannot expect him to say what you want to hear just to make you feel better. Each suggestion requires that you exert some control over your emotions. If this is impossible for you to manage at the time, then saying, "Hey, don't talk to me like that" will get your point across and is preferable to saying nothing at all. When you are criticized in public, as happened to Maria, you can

1. ignore the problem for the moment as she did,

2. repeat his inappropriate words back to him, using your sense of humor: "I'm really messing up the story because I changed the name of the turnpike?" or,

3. tell him what he's doing: "You're getting very upset about a silly story."

In private you can express your feelings and make suggestions in several ways:

1. "I'm furious at you for talking to me like that in front of our friends. If you need to correct me, then do it without criticizing me and being nasty."

2. "I feel hurt when you talk to me like that around other people. If you want to tell the story, then just say so."

3. "I'd prefer if you could appreciate my story-telling instead of looking for flaws."

Although the man in your life may be much more emotionally aware of himself than William or Tony, he may still benefit from suggestions about how to respond to *your* feelings. Ted, for instance, seems to be the opposite of these explosive men. Although he talks about his pain and anxiety all the time, he's the "man who wipes you out." Roberta, his wife of eight years, is angry when he does this but appreciates that he's never an emotional mystery to her. When he comes home from his job as an advertising manager for the local radio station, he'll warn her if he's in a bad mood and discuss his problems with her. Their conflict occurs when she needs him to listen to her after an especially exhausting day with their one-year-old son and four-year-old daughter. Not only does he not respond to her problems, he cuts her off in mid-sentence, and returns to his favorite subject—himself and his job. When Roberta screams that he is selfish and self-centered, he yells back and leaves the room. They've played out this scene many times since the children arrived. To move beyond this stalemate, Roberta needs to figure out why Ted can't listen to her, then she can suggest these feeling responses to him. Here are three possible alternatives to screaming at Ted.

1. "When you cut me off in mid-sentence, it makes me furious and I feel hurt. Can't you tell me instead that you are too overwhelmed to think about anyone but yourself right now?"

2. "I think you cut me off when I talk about the kids because you have strong feelings about me and them. I'd rather hear about those feelings than get cut off by you in mid-sentence so that you don't have to think about those feelings."

3. "I feel rejected and put down when you cut me off in the middle of talking, but I think you just don't know what to say about the problems. I would feel better if you would tell me that I'm doing a great job with the kids and that you support my decisions about them."

With each response Roberta tells Ted what she is feeling, what she thinks Ted might be feeling, and what he can say instead of storming out that will help improve their communication. If you listen to your intuition about your man, you can construct this kind of response. His intense anger usually subsides because he feels that you understand him. You'll also feel less cut off from him emotionally, less helpless, and less hopeless about the possibility of anything ever changing. But to communicate in this way you have to be aware of all the feelings you have, as well as some of his, and try to accept these emotions—for better or worse. That is not easy.

Why Is It So Hard to Know What You Feel?

Feelings affect us in powerful ways. You may not mind when love strikes, or when you feel warm and happy with another person, but you probably view most other feelings as if they were the plague. Feelings, though powerful, do not cause fevers and blisters, and despite the term "lovesick," they do not necessarily make us ill. As a matter of fact, physical illnesses are more likely to result from the suppression of feelings, or because we punish ourselves for having certain feelings, than they are from the direct and healthy expression of them. We all learned that feelings can't physically hurt us as children when we recited the rhyme, "Sticks and stones can break my bones but words can never harm me." Why is it, then, that you react to feelings as if they *could* harm you? Why is it that so many women have said to me, "Why do I have to feel this way? I don't want to feel these things," when they are talking about the man in their life. Like most of us, they don't want to accept all their feelings. They want to pick and choose the feelings they will have, like the clothes you wear or the movies you see. Yet if you can accept all your feelings, even cherish them, you will feel more confident and stronger about dealing with the man in your life.

Practice does make perfect when it comes to learning to tolerate and handle your feelings. If you are not used to living your life in touch with the full range of your emotions, you may feel overwhelmed at first. But just as you can increase your stamina for tennis or jogging, so can you develop strength and resiliency in dealing with feelings. There are several reasons why most of us don't want to have and accept our feelings, and these are based on several popular (though untrue) attitudes.

POPULAR ATTITUDE #1: THERE ARE "GOOD" AND "BAD" FEELINGS

Some feelings make us feel good, and we want those. Others make us feel bad, so why have them if we can avoid them? We decide whether or not a feeling is good by how it makes us feel about ourselves and others. From there, we go on to "choose"—to the extent that we can—which feelings we will let ourselves feel much the way we choose what foods we will eat. The big problem is that feelings are not like food. They aren't external things that we choose to take or not to take inside. If you choose not to eat chocolate ice cream one day, you've left that ice cream behind you. But when you choose not to "have" a feeling, it stays with you anyway, adding extra emotional weight, though you may not feel any different. This is what makes feeling only good feelings so appealing. It works, at least temporarily, and we are unaware of the increasing emotional weight gradually burdening us. It's also tempting to have only the "good" feelings that we are taught to have as children, so that we will be "good people." Women, of course, are especially susceptible to wanting to be "good little girls" even after they're all grown up. Being a good little girl entailed doing all the "right" things—smiling, being pleasant, showing interest in others—in other words, don't make waves. Boys, as we all know, received plaudits because they *did* make waves. As little girls, we learned to feel only those things we could express and still be good girls. Good feelings meant, and still mean to many of us, happiness, contentment, warmth toward others, loving feelings toward many. A little fear, a little anxiety, a little sadness, slight hurt, might be acceptable feelings—but only in very small degrees. We banish "bad" thoughts and feelings from our minds.

The people who were displeased by any of your strong feelings were the adult caretakers in your life—parents, teachers, baby-sitters, uncles and aunts, grandparents, and so on. You might even have been told you were *bad* when you had or expressed a feeling that *someone else* didn't want you to have. Paula was raised by her aunt and uncle who lived downstairs from her and her mother. Her father had died when she was young, so her uncle assumed his role. Tears were something he couldn't stand. Every time Paula cried, he'd threaten, "I'll give you something to cry about." Paula grew up hating her tears and thinking that the feelings that made her cry were bad, and so was she when they came to the surface. But it is as untrue to think that a feeling is bad as to think that brown hair is bad but blond hair is good. When was it that someone told you that a good girl has good feelings, while a bad girl has bad ones? If, for instance, you see anger, disappointment, impatience, and contempt as "bad" feelings, then these are probably feelings that you avoid so that you can also avoid feeling you are a bad girl for having them. Later in this chapter I will explain why it is dangerous to you and to your relationship to avoid being aware of what you feel.

Jean tried to be a good girl and have only good feelings. In her business suit and matching red lipstick and nail polish, Jean was the picture of a successful young lawyer. When she spoke of problems she was having with her boyfriend, she smiled, despite the pain she described. Jean always kept up a smile no matter what happened, but it was getting harder and harder for her to do so. Her asthma attacks had worsened since her boyfriend began talking about seeing other women. And her job never seemed to let up. She tried to be understanding of her boyfriend and never griped at work the way her colleagues did, but she couldn't stop feeling terrible recently, and burst into tears in front of her boss one day.

Until she was twenty-eight, Jean had believed that to survive she must smile. Part of the self-image she brings to adulthood is that of the good little girl. She had been sternly taught this stiff-upper-lip, chin-up lesson from her parents and from the teachers at the parochial schools she attended. She was told not to complain when she was mistreated by others, and her mother ignored her when her feelings were "too negative," though she freely criticized Jean every chance she got. Her mother and her teachers seemed to like her only when she smiled and agreed with them.

Jean was very frightened when she realized how angry she was with her boyfriend and her boss. It was as if she were still a little girl who would be punished for having a bad feeling. Accepting all your feelings as "good" ones means that you, like Jean, will accept yourself as a good person as well. This kind of self-acceptance is vital when you are trying to communicate with the man in your life, so keep in mind that there are no bad feelings, only bad (destructive) actions. Feelings do not have to lead to actions, as will be discussed later in this chapter.

POPULAR ATTITUDE #2: THERE ARE "RIGHT" AND "WRONG" FEELINGS

May Sarton, a writer and poet, once said, "It's hard to be growing up in this climate, where sex at its most crude and cold is okay, but feeling is somehow indecent." Indecent, immoral, or wrong—we talk about feelings as if they were crimes that you could be punished for. The "wrongest" of the wrong feelings, especially for women, is selfishness. For a woman to withhold something from another person, whether it's time, money, food, or emotional support, because she needs or wants to keep it for herself, is to commit a high crime. To merely *want* to be selfish (to feel but not act) is almost as serious. Consequently, many women become "overgivers" to pay for the crime they have secretly committed—feeling selfish. But overgiving leads to even more "wrong" feelings, such as feeling overburdened, resentful, disappointed, used, and, finally, angry about it all. When you decide that a feeling is wrong, you haven't eliminated the feeling, just added to it.

Nancy and Paul's life became more complicated when Nancy decided she was wrong to feel selfish and angry at Paul. Nancy has been married to Paul for five years and couldn't believe her good fortune. Paul liked to cook so much that he took care of dinner, and Nancy usually cleaned up, except on those nights when she was just too tired. Then Paul took over. Nancy marveled because Paul never complained. She knew that most of her women friends had to do everything in the kitchen—or argue all night about it. Though Nancy was in charge of the rest of the house and had to work hard to overcome Paul's resistance each time she made decorative improvements, everything Paul did still made her feel selfish. Nancy resolved to cook frequently and clean up daily to assuage her guilty conscience, but soon she resented her time in the kitchen and directed this at Paul, who said, "I never asked you to cook or clean up. As a matter of fact, I'm insulted because I don't think you like my cooking." Here's a good example of how trying to get rid of one feeling can complicate a basically simple problem. Nancy's kitchen labor didn't make her feel any better and it made Paul feel bad, and still solved nothing. When you think that a feeling you have is wrong, it is wisest to do nothing to change that feeling. Instead, try to understand why you think that such a feeling could possibly be wrong, and then remind yourself that feelings are not like the answers to a math quiz—none is right or wrong.

Many women have told me that they feel embarrassed, even humiliated, about feelings they have—when they cry from happiness, frustration, or rage, when they feel anxious or nervous, when they have sexual thoughts and fantasies. Anxiety and tears are embarrassing, they say, because they "show weakness" and someone who sees that might take advantage of them. So it is that women think of their feelings with the same John Wayne attitude that they've accused men of having for years. But embarrassment and humiliation come from outside; others make us feel that way. If you cry in front of someone who cries with you, embarrassment never enters the picture. It is not the feelings that are humiliating, but the viewer who judges them to be weak or indecent. Do *not* reveal your feelings to an unsympathetic person who will not give you the support you need. Others may say that you are weak because you have feelings—but the truth is quite the opposite. The Italian writer Anna Ortese has said that ". . . in order to feel anything you need strength." And we might add— courage.

POPULAR ATTITUDE #3: THERE ARE POPULAR AND UNPOPULAR FEELINGS

The girl who is voted "most popular" in your senior year of high school could fit in anywhere with everyone, and you, like others, may have admired her for this. Getting along with people—being popular—is a useful attribute. But chameleon-like behavior and thoughts—popularity carried to its extreme—is not. When you mimic others or feel what you think they want you to feel, you are striving for approval and love. Sometimes it is love that was denied you by parents and siblings when you were young. Sometimes it is because you faced punishment, emotional or physical, when you disagreed with the adult in charge when you were a child.

Bonnie, now a thirty-three-year-old photographer, became tongue-tied in front of her boss when he asked for her thoughts. Her boss, an opinionated, brusque man, was often critical of her suggestions, though occasionally he did give praise. Away from her boss, Bonnie was a pro—her ideas and feelings poured out—in his presence, she could only nod and agree. Although her boss was difficult, Bonnie's fear of his disapproval was small compared to her childhood fear of her father, an Air Force pilot, who demanded "perfection." Anytime she fell short of the mark, her father would banish her to her room until she could figure out what to say that would please him. Wanting to please the man in your life because you love him is part of being in a relationship. Wanting to placate someone out of fear is not. (Sometimes, however, you may decide to agree with a difficult man strategically, but that is different.)

Popularity is appealing, but be wary of the price you have to pay in denying your own sense of self. Being popular, being well liked because you agree with another person, suggests that they like themselves, not you. Here's one other example of how a desire to be popular—lovable, in this case—interfered in a relationship.

Right before their fifteenth wedding anniversary, Judy and Jack went shopping for gifts to give each other. They found two necklaces that Judy liked. One was more expensive than the other, but Judy said she liked both equally and would leave the final decision to Jack. Secretly, she hoped he would pick the more expensive necklace. When Judy opened her gift and discovered that he'd chosen the cheaper gift, her response set off a chain reaction. She accused Jack of not caring about her enough to spend the money on the more costly necklace. He was bitter and upset that she equated the amount of money he spent with how much he loved her. After the necklace issue was settled, Judy realized that she had not told Jack that she preferred the expensive gift, because she wanted him to think of her as only amiable, even if it meant her not getting what she wanted. Though she tried to avoid falling from her pedestal in his eyes by taking a necklace she didn't want and denying what she felt, it didn't work. They argued anyway, and for a few brief moments Judy was less lovable to Jack. However, they both "survived" the quarrel and learned that they could risk being unpopular with each other—even not love each other—during an argument, and then return to their loving feelings with their relationship still in one piece.

When your man accepts your unpopular feelings along with the rest of who you are that he loves, your relationship will be stronger and you will feel freer in it. Wanting to be sure that your feelings are "good," "right," and "popular" will inhibit you from knowing what it is that you feel toward your man in different situations. So that you cannot be talked out of your feelings and prevented from being the objectively feeling observer that you need to be, stop seeing your feelings as being good and bad, right and wrong, and popular and unpopular. Learn to love and understand all your feelings and help him to do the same. He will never express what he feels if you don't. You have to lead the way.

Why He Seems Irrational, or One of Us Is Crazy . . . and It's Not Me

From a piece of lint, a faint odor in the room, and a book out of place in a bookcase, Sherlock Holmes could always solve the toughest case. Seemingly crazy, unrelated clues that made no sense to anyone else made "perfect" sense to him. You have probably wished for a Sherlock Holmes to come into your life and decipher the little clues behind your man's actions or words. As irrational as he may seem at times, or as crazy as you seem to him, by doing a little of your own detective work you can get to the bottom of most of his behavior. Even the most "irrational" feelings have a logical explanation or source. You and your man have called each other "nuts" when either of you has said something the other one didn't want to hear—or, more likely, didn't understand. You each may have been strongly convinced of the other's insanity through some action—his parachute jumping or stock car racing, or getting up at 4 A.M. to go fishing. But in a more serious emotional context, he may think you're out to lunch when you tell him he's withdrawn and ignoring you. He has no idea where you got such an idea. What's wrong with you anyway? After all, he's been sitting right there in the same room with you for the whole evening watching television. Or perhaps he's accused you of flirting with a man at a party and you tell him, this time, that *he's* nuts. You don't even know which man he's talking about. At times like these, wouldn't it be great to convene a judge and jury to hear both your sides and then tell him that his is indeed "off in left field." In your fantasy, order and sanity will be restored, and *he* will know to not do or say those things again. Even if such a fantastic event were to occur, winning the case would not help your relationship. Except for specific instances where behavior threatens your safety and his (in which case stopping the behavior takes priority over talking about it; drinking and driving, committing violence, using dangerous drugs would fall in this category) calling each other "irrational" shuts down all communication. Your goal is to open up your communication, so you'll need to understand where all feelings come from—yours and his. Once you do this, you can gradually accept that even deep, dark "yucky" feelings are not going to harm anyone.

When you are in a relationship, your and his feelings combine and multiply in leaps and bounds. One plus one equals two, then four, then eight, and so on. Sometimes the feelings between the two of you seem more like a forest fire that is raging out of control. Part of the chemistry of love that scientists have tried to measure is certainly composed of feelings. When Catherine, a twenty-eight-year-old woman, discusses the frustration she feels about her boyfriend, Sam, she is quick to add that there is "something that draws us together—an intensity. I don't know exactly what it's about, but it goes very deep. I know I should break up with him, but there's passion there too." That intense "something that draws us together" are feelings. Though they often cause trouble, without them there is no relationship. "I don't feel anything for him anymore" is usually the harbinger of an imminent breakup. At first glance our feelings seem not to be governed by laws of logic—they just "happen." You can feel depressed on a picnic with friends under a brilliantly blue sky and happy at home when your day's plans have been rained out. You may even have felt "lonely in a crowd." Yet despite the irrational appearance of so many of our feelings, each of them is extremely logical—all can be traced to plausible explanations either in the present or in the early childhood experiences that have left strong impressions even when you may not actually remember what happened, or when, or with whom.

No one was more confused by her jumbled feelings than Maggie. After a wonderful weekend with her boyfriend, Sam, who finally wined and dined her, she became very anxious. In the years before, when he was rarely available to meet her needs she had wanted him desperately. Maggie has had to be quite strong to deal with Sam's antics. They met in an art class two years ago. He's an art director with an ad agency, and she is a weekend painter. Maggie stays at Sam's loft on the weekends, where the light is bright, and they paint together, but during the week they stay in her apartment. She's learned to live with the fact that even though they've been committed to each other for over a year and are planning to wed, he refuses to take the key to her apartment. This has caused problems for them both on mornings when she has to be at work before he does. They've had numerous fights about this and now she feels he's just crazy. Sam could offer no rational explanation for not taking Maggie's key. Maybe because of this key problem, or maybe because Sam's making a commitment, Maggie now feels more anxious and depressed than she did when she thought they might break up.

When we look at Sam's childhood, the reason behind his strange behavior over the key is clear. Sam's mother always worked and he had to let himself in at home and remain inside until she got home. One day when he lost his key he was happy to join his friends to play and arrived home after his mother did. Without listening to his explanation, she screamed at him and then gave him the silent treatment for the next three days. This has left him with a negative attitude about handling keys (and about women), even though Maggie's not his mother and would not treat him that way. If Maggie understands that there is a "real" reason for Sam's refusal to accommodate her on this point, she can react to his "craziness" differently. She does *not* even have to know the exact cause. All she needs to do is recognize that deep down something is upsetting Sam that doesn't make sense to her and may not make sense even to him. Here's what you can and cannot do when your man has an unreasonable reaction that confuses and angers you.

1. Do *not* yell or get into a heated argument and try to convince him that he is being irrational.

2. *Always* acknowledge that he has a right to the way he feels.

3. Try one of these dialogues:

   a. "What you are doing is upsetting to me. I'm sure you have a reason for acting this way. But it's causing a problem for us. What should we do about the problem?"

   b. Or take a firm but not bossy stand to protect yourself without acting resentful—do not participate in the unreasonable behavior and say, "I'm leaving the key for you to lock the door when you leave. I know you don't like this but I don't want to argue and be late for work again. And you know it's unsafe to leave the door unlocked."

When you act this way you are also showing your mate how you would want to be treated if the situation were reversed and you seemed irrational to him. For example, Sam felt hurt and angry because Maggie does not appear happy and excited about their wedding plans, especially because she has wanted this for a long time. He is also confused and feels like he will never make her happy. As far as Sam is concerned, Maggie seems "off her rocker." Sam might withdraw, act sullen, or get angry and lecture her to "figure out what she wants already." *Or* he can try the alternative approach I will call "deep understanding."

1. Acknowledge (to himself) that Maggie seems unreasonable and that "something else" must be the cause.

2. Tell her that he understands that she feels this way.

3. State how he feels (hurt, angry).

4. Ask Maggie for reassurance that marriage to him is what she wants.

71

The "something else" that makes Maggie depressed and anxious when she should be elated lies in her family history too. Maggie is used to having to fend for herself. Physically abused by her mother and ignored by her stepfather, she expects to be mistreated and left alone. Now that Sam has come around to treating her well, she has to get used to it, just as you'd have to adjust to a warm climate after years of living in the cold. Also, as Sam treats her better, she will really begin to feel what she missed growing up without the love she needed, and may experience a delayed sense of loss. Sam does not have to know all these details to acknowledge that Maggie has a right to "irrational" feelings. All that he, and you, have to do is to understand what the English writer Stevie Smith once said: ". . . you can suffer just as much for something that isn't real as for something that is." Though one of you is having feelings that don't seem real to the other, you are both still suffering.

One last example of how "irrational" feelings develop between two people is what happened to Betty and Marty. Betty and Marty, who married five years ago, are both in their late thirties. This is Betty's first marriage and Marty's second; Betty has been involved seriously before. Having seen other relationships fail, they are both committed to talking about what they feel when they are having problems. But they're both confused by their recent fights. They always seem to occur the morning after they've made love the night before. Marty starts it by acting angry and impatient with Betty, or walking around silently as if he's looking for a fight. Betty feels irritated and dissatisfied with him, and lonely when he acts this way. Their fights burst the bubble of happiness that tender lovemaking creates.

It seems irrational for a man who has just enjoyed a mutually pleasurable night with his woman to be so angry and dissatisfied with her the very next morning, especially when nothing particularly bad has happened to precipitate these feelings. This "get-close-and-run-away" pattern, also called approach-avoidance, is quite common and happens not just after making love, but after a wonderful night at the opera or dancing till dawn. Some people, as we discussed in the chapter on commitment, run far away due to fear. Men and women who are in a relationship, however, give each other the flexibility to feel angry, irritable, dissatisfied, and lonely for what seems like no reason or crazy reasons, but still maintain the relationship. Marty has his specific reasons for his behavior, though in the heat of the argument he is not consciously aware of why he is picking on Betty. Sullenness and impatience are reactions Marty saw frequently at home. His father always scowled at his mother, though he wasn't sure why. His father never seemed to like it much when Marty got along with his mother, either, so Marty talked to her only when his father wasn't around. When Marty acts so unpleasantly over nothing, he is doing what he learned would get his father's approval. Fortunately, he is not like this all the time. But whenever he has been tender with Betty—which means that he has been intimate with someone outside his nuclear family—he feels compelled to "return home" and do it his father's way again. It is almost as if his father had been watching the night before and knew that Marty had been tender, so Marty feels obliged to let Dad know he's still with him. Marty feels anxious when he's been close to Betty.

Whenever the man in your life acts in crazy ways or expresses crazy feelings, slow down and proceed with caution. Since these kinds of feelings occur so unexpectedly, it is easy to go full speed ahead into a pointless argument.

For example, when Joe responded angrily each time he and Mary went into an expensive restaurant, Mary tried to talk him out of his mood. He would criticize the service, the other customers (especially wealthy-looking ones), and generally seem morose. When Mary tried to convince Joe that he should relax and enjoy himself, or would tell him that there was nothing wrong with the service, it would spark an argument that lasted through dinner and all the way home. Once Mary saw that trying to "make sense" didn't make sense to Joe, she instead talked to him about the problem when he was in a better mood. She suggested that they go only to restaurants of his choosing (she noticed she had picked out most of the problem places) because it wasn't fun for her if it wasn't fun for him. Joe seemed relieved. Mary also privately decided that if this strange behavior happened again, she would leave the restaurant, with or without Joe, rather than sit through another upsetting meal.

Mary doesn't really need to know that Joe's problem stems from the guilt he feels for having left his poor background behind and being able now to afford to dine out with the rich folks. Mary only has to

1. Be alert to a strange behavior and feelings.

2. Remove herself from the argument.

3. Decide not to try to change Joe's mind.

4. Devise a plan of action that will protect her from another disruptive night out.

When you decide to communicate this way with your man about irrational feelings, you are showing how much you care about him and your relationship, and that you accept him, crazy moods and all. Of course you will also want to have him accept your "crazy times." As difficult as it is to watch the man you love express feelings that make no sense to you, you must resist trying to convince him that he is wrong. Since irrational feelings are often "situational"—brought on by a specific situation—it is best for you to leave the scene temporarily if you are too upset to stay detached from what your mate is feeling. When you remove yourself in this way, you not only avert a fruitless argument, you emphasize to him how disruptive his behavior is. Here, then, is a summary of what to do, and not do when he seems "irrational" to you.

Dos

1. Be aware that most people have feelings that seem crazy to others, yet there is always some explanation in the past.

2. Acknowledge his right to his feelings, whatever they are.

3. Recognize what you feel toward him.

4. Remove yourself from a distressing situation if you feel that you will get involved and argumentative or if you are suffering emotionally.

5. Tell him what you are doing and why. Be firm.

6. At a calmer time, discuss what you and he feel can be done to prevent reoccurrences.

DON'TS

1. Do not get into a heated argument or try to convince him that he is being crazy.

2. Do not assume that he will always be like this, or that one crazy episode makes him a crazy person.

3. Do not remain in a situation that is upsetting you.

4. Do not remain where you will be forced into a pointless argument.

Anger: Not to Be Ignored

We all experience anger whether we like it or not. In its most intense state, the feeling lasts for a few seconds. Like an x-ray, it flashes through our mind and body. Anger is one of many feelings that we can experience in our unconscious mind and in our physical bodies though we may not realize that we are angry, or jealous, or depressed. People around you may see that you are angry from the glare in your eyes, your flushed cheeks, your rapid breathing, or your clenched jaw.

Or they may think you ought to be angry (they would be in your shoes), but still *you* don't think you are. What allows you to be so oblivious of something that another person feels or sees in you so plainly is one of the most common defense mechanisms, denial. You deny to yourself and to others that you have any feeling toward a particular person or situation. Anger is the feeling we most often deny, with jealousy, hurt, and loving feelings running a close second. Men and women deny anger equally, but their reasons differ. Men are more often concerned that if they admit to and experience an angry feeling when it first arises, they will do something violent, be "out of control." A man who as many as fifteen years before went against someone in anger may have been so frightened by the experience that he tries never to feel angry again. Even if the man hurt no one, he may carry this fear of losing control forever. Women also deny their angry feelings because they are afraid of becoming violent, though to a much lesser degree than men. Women are most often concerned that they will be disliked, or, worse, abandoned, by another person if they feel and express angry feelings. Men, of course, share this fear also. But although we might all want to wipe out anger, have our days be filled with laughter and smiles, denying angry feelings toward your man has the disastrous effect of cooling down your love for him. What happened to Peter and Lois could happen to you.

Lois was a determined woman who had worked her way up in the telecommunications business. She was proud of her sales record and the long hours she put in to get where she was. Pete, an accountant in a city office, was not ambitious at all. He denied being angry or even upset about Lois's long work hours during the six years they were married. Lois, meanwhile, ignored Pete's black moods. She seemed to not care that Pete was often depressed, withdrawn, and unavailable to her. It was not surprising then when Lois began an affair almost under Pete's nose. Their confrontation when Pete discovered the affair nearly became violent, and Lois moved out soon after.

Both Peter and Lois admitted that they had not felt much love toward the other in the last year they were married. They each harbored unspoken resentments and furious feelings toward the other that they denied and suppressed until the cork blew. People who are full of anger find it hard to be loving. In Peter and Lois's case, there was little love left to salvage by the time it was over.

As you can see, the avoidance of anger through denial can kill love. Because Lois had been beaten as a child, she assumed that violence was the only way to express anger. She thought she was protecting herself by denying the feeling. Pete had been abandoned in childhood by his alcoholic mother, who would run to a bar whenever she was angry. He grew up thinking that the best way to deal with anger was to avoid it altogether. Having never learned more constructive ways of handling anger, they denied it.

In another case, the woman's refusal to express her anger destroyed her relationship. Ruth and Ira looked like brother and sister; both are tall with blond curly hair. During the year they had lived together, Ruth made herself available to Ira at all times, to the point that her own friendships suffered. She denied that she was upset by his constant demands and possessiveness of her, but one day the dam burst and Ruth began making her own plans with old friends. When she wasn't home in the evening a few times, Ira became nasty, calling her selfish and warning her that he didn't want a relationship where she was out all the time. Ruth immediately made plans to move out. She could see no way to spend time with her friends and have a relationship with Ira. Besides, she thought Ira was right—she *was* selfish.

Ira is a man who controls people with his anger, or tries to anyway. Ruth has been angry with Ira for the year they've been together, but she denies this vehemently, right through to the day that she packs her bags. Her real reason for ending the relationship so abruptly is that she does not want to be angry with Ira. Unconsciously, she is more afraid to fight it out with him than to leave him. As her buried anger increased, her loving feelings decreased. By walking away from Ira and their relationship, Ruth is rejecting an opportunity to stick up for herself as she never could at home when her mother told her she was selfish because she made her own plans. This is the third long-term relationship that she has left because she denied her anger at being criticized and did not think she had the right to stand up for what she wanted. No wonder she feels that she loses herself when she's with a man. When you deny your anger, you also deny your innermost self.

Women and men are also inhibited from expressing their anger toward each other because they are confused about what *is* a constructive way to express their feelings. Many women on the receiving end of anger do not know how and when to verbally protect themselves because they do not even realize when they are being criticized or really attacked verbally. It is important, then, to examine the different ways to express anger so that you can become an expert in knowing when you have been "attacked" with your man's anger or perhaps when you have been provocative.

NONVERBAL WAYS OF EXPRESSING ANGER

1. Silence. The first possibility of how you might respond to feeling angry is to ignore the feeling—either consciously or unconsciously. Denial, suppression, and repression help us to ignore the feeling. You may not be at all aware that you have just felt angry, or you may choose to forget it and not say anything.

2. Acting Out. We know that acting out is another way to express anger. This can mean that you do something physical to demonstrate your anger—break a plate, slam garbage can covers, and in the extreme form cause physical injury to yourself or another person. Acting out can also mean taking an action that is, either consciously or not, designed to cause another person emotional pain. Although having affairs is a common form of acting out in relationships, chronically showing up late every time you're supposed to meet, or being a workaholic, or being irresponsible about money all accomplish the same goal: They show the other person that you are angry at them without you having to say what you feel directly. Other than breaking a plate now and then, or slamming doors, the other forms of acting out inhibit

closeness and put a halt to meaningful emotional communication of anger and all other feelings.

3. Physical Illness. When you become ill instead of experiencing feelings, you are somatizing. Somatization, although effective in getting you to take care of him, also can have a disastrous effect on the expression of anger —yours and his. Closeness can develop during illness, but it can be at tragic cost to one's health. This kind of closeness lacks a healthy passion.

4. Sublimation. Still another way to express anger without saying anything is through channeling your energy into constructive activities. This is known as sublimation. Many people find physical activity a productive way to discharge angry feelings. Karate, jogging, boxing, aerobics, and other forms of vigorous physical exercise let us "work it off." (Note: Using exercise to avoid your mate because you are scared to say what you feel or you don't know how is not productive.) A passionate interest in politics or painting, bird-watching or playing the guitar can also serve to sublimate one's anger.

Verbal Ways We Express Anger

1. Criticism. The most common verbal expression of anger is criticism. The words "anger," "annoyed," or "irritated," are never actually spoken. Instead, we list the other person's faults and problems as we see them. "You've never cared about anyone but yourself ever since I've known you." "You're the biggest slob, but I'm the one who has to do all the work around here. Are you so out of it that you don't see the mess you make?"

These types of statements may sound familiar to you. How harsh it sounds depends on one's tone of voice. Another example, often said by men to women, is "Are you gaining weight? That dress looks awful on you." Or "You know how to spend money but not how to save it. You don't care what I have to go through to keep our heads above water." Criticism can also take the form of a lecture, like the kind parents give their teenagers. Frequently partners lecture each other when they are angry or scared or hurt, secretly hoping that the lecture will stop whatever was done or said that caused you pain.

One other way that you may criticize him or he you is by "playing therapist." Analysis of each other's flaws, like all forms of criticism, often only angers or hurts the other person, even if the analysis is correct. He may say, for instance, "You know the reason that you're always late is that your family could never be on time either." Or "With a mother like yours, it's no wonder you act so crazy." Or "You don't stand up to your boss because you could never stand up to your family either. You just want everybody to love you."

People who are criticized—no matter who does it or how it is done—feel angry or worse and often want to retaliate. Sometimes yelling criticisms at each other helps clear the air for a more productive discussion later. (Caution: This works only if both have participated equally in the exchange. One person screaming at a silent partner does not qualify as being helpful.) Many women need practice to recognize when they have been criticized or have been critical of someone else. One woman was criticized for so much as a child that when her boyfriend would analyze her faults, she believed it was "for her own good." Instead of protesting his behavior and defending herself, she became depressed. Once she knew that he was critical and this was bad for her—and for their relationship—she would stop him as soon as he started by saying, "You are criticizing me, and I don't like it. Stop now before we really get into a fight." Eventually he learned to follow her example and would tell her the same thing when she had started in on him out of anger. You can more constructively express what you feel and head toward an understanding and resolution of the problem only after all criticism has stopped. First become alert to the sound of criticism—yours and his.

2. **Verbal Attacks.** Critical comments taken a step further fall into the category of verbal attacks in which anything goes in an argument, verbally, that is—insults of all sorts, four-letter words, sarcasm. It's as if the internal censor who usually screens our words is on vacation. You and your mate sound like cab drivers at an accident scene. When Ida, a bank vice-president, lost the pictures from their trip after showing them in her office, her husband, George, saw red. "I can't believe you can be so dumb—maybe you're getting senile," he yelled. Name-calling, cursing, and other forms of attack may occur when either or both of you are frustrated with a problem that never seems to change. Perhaps you had been keeping it all inside until the feelings explode. Other times, however, you may have learned that this is the way that most people fight by watching your parents at home. Or, as in George's case, his mother was too permissive and let him yell at her. George does not

know that his way of expressing anger is destructive and this is the way that he now yells at Ida. Even in a free-for-all, where both of you are on the attack, no one escapes unhurt.

Although an occasional fight can clear the air, both of you must be sure to apologize afterward to heal the rift. As with criticism, recognize the sound of an attacking comment and stop it at the beginning.

The Better Ways: Constructive Ways to Express Anger

There are ways to say you're angry without criticizing or remaining silent or having an affair, or breaking a plate or someone's arm. This more productive way to express what you each feel when you're upset takes thought, work, and practice. You must be willing to heed this advice given by Charlotte Bronte in *Jane Eyre*.

The passions may rage furiously, like true heathens, as they are; and the desires may imagine all sorts of vain things, but judgment shall still have the last word in every argument, and the casting vote in every decision.

To be both passionate and aware of what you are saying and how it will affect him, and also what he is saying and how it affects you, is a skill developed only through trial and error. This constructive approach is made up of three parts:

1. State your feelings

2. Identify what was done or said that was upsetting, and

3. Tell him what you would like him to say or do differently.

For instance, you are waiting for him at home, two hours after he was supposed to meet you there before going out to dinner. He has not called but finally walks in extremely apologetic because of a problem at work and heavy traffic. You are furious, hungry, hurt, and scared. One constructive way to express yourself is to say, "I get furious at you when you don't bother to call and let me know you'll be late. I also got worried that something terrible had happened to you. You've got to call me and let me know what's going on or perhaps we shouldn't make any advance plans." Another way to tell him that you are even more enraged is "When you mistreat me like this, I feel like ripping you apart. I feel so frustrated because you are so inconsiderate. It seemed like you didn't really want to go out to dinner tonight." You, like the many women I have worked with, may be surprised to know that saying "I feel like ripping you apart" (or hitting you or killing you) is not a destructive expression of your feelings. It conveys the intensity of your feelings and the passion that you feel toward your man and saying it will immediately relieve you of your anger.

However, saying "I feel" is different from saying "I want to hurt you." Because "I want" states that you might take this action, this kind of communication is destructive to your relationship and to you. Similarly, saying "I'm going to physically hurt you if . . ." is a threat, and threats of physical violence as a way of controlling another person are dangerous and break off all meaningful communication. These latter two forms of relating must be eliminated if you and he want to be able to say what you feel. You must keep violence and threats of violence out of your life. Physical abuse of any kind—by either of you—indicates that counseling is indicated.

MISUSE OF ANGER: VIOLENCE AND THE LIFETIME ANGRY COUPLE

Newspapers and TV news frequently carry reports of people who suffer, and even die, at the hands of someone who expressed their anger through physical violence. Battered wives, battered children, even battered husbands, are familiar topics. For most of us, however, expressing anger by taking physical action means grabbing and shaking your mate or landing the occasional punch on the arm. Even in this mild form, physical violence is harmful. People resort to violence when they reach an extreme point of frustration. Most frequently, it is the woman who is frustrated because she feels she cannot "get through" to her man, that he is not responding to her needs, and that he has "tuned her out." The man, in this case, most often feels that he is totally inadequate to improve this situation, a feeling he does not like having, and for which he blames the woman's demands. If he can only "shut her up," he can stop feeling inadequate.

Rhoda and Carlos are in this spot. Carlos, who is from a large Spanish-speaking family, saw his father go out with the guys every Friday night, and sometimes Sunday night as well. It was natural, then, for Carlos to do the same thing when he got older. When Rhoda married him, she knew about these evenings out and didn't especially like them, but she assumed it would change. After a year, however, she could see that she was having little influence on Carlos. He would break plans with her, and go out with the guys. One Friday Rhoda felt especially lonely and asked Carlos to stay home. When he refused, Rhoda could not stop herself from pursuing the topic. Finally, when Carlos began to leave for the evening, she tried to block his way and he pushed her so that she fell, slightly hurting her hand, but scaring her even more.

Most women have felt Rhoda's frustration at some time, though the events may differ. Feeling ignored, unloved, and "pushed away," you fight back to stop these awful feelings. Sometimes the woman was hit out of anger by parents as a child or watched another child get hit. Sometimes it is the man's family that has a history of physical violence. An encounter like the one between Rhoda and Carlos stirs up early feelings about being abandoned, unloved, and misunderstood. Obviously, regardless of how Rhoda feels, she should *never* physically stop Carlos, and he should never push her. What she can do is to make her own plans with friends for those evenings. She might, if she wants, tell Carlos that he is welcome to come along if he'd like, which will show Carlos that she can be separate but also care about him—something he did not learn watching his father. One of the reasons for Carlos's rigid behavior is that he is terrified of being helplessly dependent and losing himself in a woman's needs. This fear obscures his usual loving feelings for Rhoda, especially when he feels trapped. If Rhoda wants to pursue this issue with Carlos, she must discuss his evening out at another time, preferably when they are both calm.

George Eliot, in her novel *The Mill on the Floss,* writes, "Anger and jealousy can no more bear to lose sight of their objects than love." You can see how true this statement is when you encounter a couple trapped together for a lifetime of anger. Though their life together might seem unbearable to you, these couples could neither tolerate being apart—nor being happy together. You may have heard them seated in a restaurant or standing behind you on the movie line. They sound as if they hate each other, with their constant nagging and picking. And they do hate each other—but that's only part of the story. They also need each other deeply, the same way that Archie needed Edith in *All in the Family,* Ralph needed Alice in *The Honeymooners,* and Oscar needed Felix in *The Odd Couple* (and vice versa). Deep down, although each partner blames the other for their unhappy life, they feel that none better would want them; that they don't deserve a less argumentative, more supportive partner, a better life. Often one of them sees nothing wrong: constant anger and a lack of warmth are a way of life. The roots often run back to a childhood that was similarly without expressions of love and was riddled by criticism. In fact, replacing this meager, loveless diet too suddenly with one rich in love (as well as anger) can sometimes cause a person to become ill.

The gradual enhancement of intimacy is easier to learn to deal with, whether we are working it out with a longtime partner, or a new one.

ANGER—YOUR PARTNER IN SETTING LIMITS

Just as a leopard's sense of smell alerts her to danger, so you can use your angry feelings to alert you to the need for changes in your relationship. First, of course, you must be aware of your own anger. You can then assess what it is that is producing these feelings—both from your past and your present. And finally, you can communicate what the problem is, and what you need, to your man. As you'll recall, Ira was a controlling man who didn't want Ruth to see her friends. They broke up because Ruth could not use her angry feelings to set necessary limits with Ira regarding the way he spoke to her. When Ira told her she was selfish for seeing her friends and then threatened to end the relationship if she continued to make her own plans, Ira was attacking, criticizing, and threatening Ruth with his anger. Instead of running scared, Ruth could have told Ira that it was not okay for him to use his angry feelings like this. She might have said, "I can understand that you are angry and scared because I'm doing something new by seeing my friends instead of spending all my time with you. But you cannot attack and call me names and threaten me like that. I want a relationship with you where we can be separate as well as together, otherwise neither of us will be happy. I still love you and will not leave you just because I'm seeing my friends too." This complicated communication tells Ira several things that he did not know before:

1. He can be angry but not destructive in the way he expresses himself.

2. He is not only angry but scared that Ruth will leave him.

3. Ruth loves him and he is reassured that she is staying despite his threats.

4. A healthy relationship must allow for separateness as well as closeness.

In cases like Ira's, anger often masquerades for other feelings that we don't want to have because they make us appear unsafe and vulnerable. The fear of being left by Ruth, for example, is a feeling that Ira would not "admit to" because he is afraid he would fall apart, or Ruth might take advantage of him. He feels safer encased in his anger, protected, he thinks, by his rage. If you can use your emotional x-ray vision to peer beneath his angry feelings, you will see how much he needs you and you will be more confident. It may seem that it takes the wisdom of Solomon to love a difficult man, but most of the women I have worked with have learned to use their natural gifts—their intuition and their feelings (especially anger)—to construct a strong framework on which their relationship can grow.

Saying Those Sweet Nothings:
The Man Who Doesn't Nurture

How do I love thee?
Let me count the ways
—ELIZABETH BARRETT BROWNING

We fell out, my wife and I.
O we fell out I know not why,
And kiss'd again with tears.
And blessings on the falling out
That all the more endears.
When we fall out with those we love
And kiss again with tears!
—ALFRED, LORD TENNYSON

WOMEN are often nurturing to a fault. They don't know when to stop giving, yet their man doesn't know how to start (nurturing, that is). We have observed how anger, when withheld, can eat away at love and destroy a couple.

The same is true of anger's opposite—love. When love is withheld, relationships can turn sour and wither, as happened to Paulette.

Paulette, thirty-four, has admired Casey, thirty-six, from the day she met him five years ago. She knew he was smart because he was an engineer but he also was an opera buff, and Paulette told him outright how impressed she was by what he knew. For the first year, Casey also admired Paulette's talents and encouraged her whenever she needed it. In the beginning, after they married, they were always doing nice things for each other and appreciated each other openly. Slowly, however, life changed. When Paulette came home enthusiastic about her job as real estate broker, Casey was either silent or barely happy for her whereas before he would tell her how great she was. He rarely complimented Paulette about her appearance anymore either, although in the first year he even wrote her love sonnets. Paulette read Casey's silence as an accusation that he didn't find her as attractive or terrific as she used to be. Sometimes she felt terrible and depressed about this; other times she felt angry and hated him because he no longer seemed to be the man she had married. Casey didn't even laugh at her jokes as much as he used to, even though Paulette still laughed at his. She had tried to stop being too supportive of him, but it's her nature to be positive with people even when they didn't reciprocate. Was that wrong? she wondered. Other men she worked with began to appeal to her because at least they were interested in and flattered her, but she didn't want to do anything that would jeopardize her marriage. What she wanted was that Casey should go back to his former self, but she didn't know how to make that happen.

Casey has become a man who doesn't nurture. He has forgotten that a vital ingredient in any relationship is "positive stroking." Although many couples don't survive because they don't fight, just as many break up because they never make up. Positive stroking, besides making you feel good for the moment, is the stuff that holds your relationship together through the many difficult moments of working on your problems. In this chapter we will examine the various kinds of positive attention you should expect him to give you, why he doesn't, and how to get him to be supportive and loving. We will also look at why you don't ask for what you want. As always, you will have to show him through your example how to use sweet nothings to pull you through the angry times.

Shakespeare told us that

My bounty is as boundless as the sea,
My love as deep; the more I give to thee,
The more I have, for both are infinite

and many people in love act this way. Men who don't nurture, however, act as if the more they give to you the less they'll have for themselves. When you love a difficult man, you often feel more anger than love, more disappointment than understanding, more contempt than admiration. Your love does not feel deep and infinite; in fact, it seems to have disappeared altogether. Once your anger has passed, however, reminding yourself and your mate that love and other positive feelings still exist between you will help in the following ways.

1. It will emotionally balance the previous negative exchange between you and change the "tone." After you have aired your feelings, you will need to change the climate. Telling each other something positive or at least changing your approach to a warm, friendly one will help.

2. Say "I love you." You will also remind each other that you still care, even though you have been angry. You are telling each other that you want to stay together and continue to improve the relationship. The bond between you is reconnected.

3. Most of us learned "all-or-nothing" unconscious messages about anger, such as "No one will love you if you're angry," "You will be abandoned if you are angry," "You are a completely bad, unkind monster for being angry," and so on. When you say positive things to your man and he to you, you are offsetting these early powerful warnings that anger and love cannot coexist in a successful relationship and establishing that here both feelings can, and do, exist.

Positive stroking should not be reserved only for after an argument. "Sweet nothings" must be sprinkled throughout your days—and nights—together, in good times and bad. Couples who are stingy with words of love and support are less likely to survive when the going gets rough. Joan and Arthur's situation provides a good example of how a strong relationship bears up under pressure.

Joan, a fashion illustrator, has always been close to her parents. They live only a few blocks away from where she and Arthur, her husband of twelve years, have an apartment. Nurturing each other has been a top priority for Joan and Arthur since they met when Arthur was a struggling writer and Joan had just finished art school. Each is proud of the other's accomplishments, and compliments like "I love you," "You're great," and "I'm a lucky guy (gal)" flow between them. But last year a serious conflict developed after Joan's father died and her mother suddenly became totally dependent on her. After running between their two homes, Joan decided to bring her mother to live with them. Arthur was dead set against this, feeling that he'd lose his wife and the privacy of his home. Joan, who was feeling guilt ridden, became furious at Arthur, and they argued over this for weeks. After especially fierce discussions, however, they would tell each other how much they still cared and even apologize if they had been insulting. Gradually Joan began to see Arthur's point of view, and arranged for a housekeeper and weekly visits with her mother. Arthur made sure to let Joan know that he appreciated and admired her for setting limits with her mother. Joan's mother seemed to benefit from this too. She became more self-sufficient and began to go out by herself.

Arthur does not withhold his warm feelings from Joan, and she is always caring toward him. The loving feelings actually make it safe for them to express their anger freely and to have different opinions. The repeated expressions of their positive feelings during both easy periods and crises strengthen a bond they can rely on during difficult times. The man who doesn't nurture misses these frequent opportunities in his day-to-day life to say the sweet nothings that are really everything. We will look at the underlying reasons why this happens, but first let's examine what these opportunities are, and the different ways that lovers can warm each other with words.

What Is Positive Stroking? Let Us Count the Ways

There are numerous misconceptions about what it means to show warmth and support to another person. Some men mistake expressing gratitude—thank-yous—for expressions of warm feelings, while others think a look, either sexual or loving, is worth a thousand words. Finally, there are those who communicate telepathically. "I don't have to tell her how wonderful she is. She *knows* how I feel." If you are in a relationship with a man whose verbal repertoire of positive strokes is limited to the above, you know how deprived you can feel when the right words are never said. Your relationship and you require nurturing. Attachment behaviors between mothers and children is the prototype for all attachments that we develop as adults. Nancy Chodorow, in her book *The Reproduction of Motherhood,* tells us that attachments between individuals develop "in response to the quality of interaction, and not (in response) to having primary physiological needs met." This is good news for women. Instead of forming an attachment to your man in the ancient ways of women (cooking, housekeeping, etc.), it is more likely that you will create a lasting bond with your man through emotional relating—verbal expressions of feeling. And you must teach him to do as you do. Positive stroking in combination with other feelings (anger, frustration, anxiety, and so on) are the vital components of a strong and healthy attachment.

What, then, are the ways that you can verbally express your warmth and support to him, and get him to say the same to you? Although the categories we will discuss are probably familiar to you, most of the women I have worked with do not realize that they are entitled to get this kind of attention from their man, and that they must give it in return.

1. Appreciation. Defined as "to value greatly . . . to enjoy with intelligence (as in the appreciation of good poetry)," appreciation can be expressed many ways. Any time you do some chore, plan an evening out, remember an important event in his life, or listen sympathetically to his day's toil is an occasion for him to say "I appreciate that you . . ." You, meanwhile, can use appreciation to encourage him each time he expresses feelings as you have asked him to, such as when he communicates his anger in a direct manner without being critical. Or maybe when he cooperates in doing something that he did not want to do and did only for you, such as visiting your family with you. You, of course, deserve appreciation for the favors that you do for him and for the efforts that you make to keep the feelings flowing in a constructive way. He should appreciate that you have done something that enhances the feeling of unity between you. It is a thank-you that warmly expresses the value that he places on you (and you on him) because of the efforts that you both put forth on behalf of your relationship.

2. Admiration. Théophile Gautier, a nineteenth-century writer, said, "To love is to admire with the heart; to admire is to love with the mind." Admiration often exists during the early infatuation stage of love but

quickly fades as infatuation becomes adult love. Admiration has been short-changed in relationships because we grow up to regard it as an "all-or-nothing" emotion. Women and men have mistakenly thought that they must admire or be admired totally rather than for specific traits. We might add that you can admire "at certain moments about specific characteristics" while at the same time disliking elements of the same person. Admiration differs from appreciation in that he does not admire what you have done for *him* but he admires who you are and what you have done separately from the relationship. He may admire the way you dress, your bowling skills, or your ability to deal effectively with a difficult client at work, just as you admire his dexterity on the dance floor or his ability to fix the stereo system. Admiring each other may mean acknowledging that one of you is "better than" the other in a certain area, and this is the first step in being able to learn from each other. Men, especially, resist learning new skills from their mates. When you feel admired you feel enhanced as an individual, not as a part of a couple. Because of this, he may hold back admiration if he is afraid that you will get to be "too good for him" and leave him. Of course, the opposite is true: The more you are admired and admire him, the more reason to stay together. Arguing couples who are disappointed in their relationship quickly forget what they admired in each other when they met, which is sad, since troubled times are when they should be remembering these things.

3. Praise. Of all the sweet nothings, praise is everyone's favorite and the easiest way to give positive stroking.

Praise is usually given because of a particular attribute or skill or achievement. He says you are "smart, beautiful, clever, talented, sexy, or highly capable." Perhaps *he* is terrific because he has been made a vice-president, or you have just written a "brilliant" article and are great in his eyes. You are praised because of your own personal attributes, but praise differs from admiration in that the implication that the "praiser" wishes he might be like you and feels somewhat inferior is not there, as it can be in admiration.

Well-meant praise should be a gift. Most of us glow when we are sincerely praised. But praise brings with it other complications because it is so often given by parental figures: parents, bosses, teachers. When it is *not* forthcoming from these authority figures, it is yearned for. When the dictionary defines praise as "to honor in words; approval expressed in words," the word "approval" further reminds you of a grading system. Shakespeare even told us that "our praises are our wages," and you may recall instances in which you accepted praise in lieu of money for your services. Because of this connection, you may feel that there is an underlying expectation—a string—attached to any praise you receive—the expectation that you will "keep up the good work." Though this often happens with authority figures, it rarely occurs when he praises you (or you praise him). You may still feel that there's an attendant expectation anyway. You are especially susceptible to equating praise with expectations if you were the good kid who always did the right thing for approval but never felt that you were loved for yourself—as is, without the accomplishments. As a result of feeling that you are not loved for yourself and that constant achievement is necessary, you (or he) may react to praise from each other with anger or even depression at times. Generally feelings like these are a by-product of your history with your family. If they occur, try to determine whether your family misused praise or whether your man really is expecting something back when he praises you.

One last warning about praise: Genuine praise shimmers and bubbles; forced praise falls flat, as you probably know. Alexander Pope's well-known expression "damn with faint praise" says it all. Thus it is important that any praise offered be authentic. If you doubt whether he was sincere, or if he doubts you, ask.

4. Affection. This is a sweet, gentle feeling, as one friend might feel for another, as your aunt may have felt for you, as you may feel toward a fellow employee or toward a friend's child. A pat on the head, a warmly clasped hand, a tender hug—these are all physical expressions of affection. Sharing a good laugh, or remembering an important moment, are situations you associate with people for whom you feel affection. The definition of affection, "love, a liking (for, of)," tells you that you can express affection toward someone you like, or even love, but without the intensity of a romantic love. Does this mean, then, that he should not feel affection for you if he also feels more intense love? Hopefully not. You probably want to be liked for yourself as much as you want to be intensely loved, and affection (in words or with hugs) is the best way to show liking.

Affection is the kind of attention you may have received from your parents, or else wanted if it wasn't forthcoming. You wanted to be smiled at and played with by someone who seemed to be enjoying you completely with no strings attached. As a child this helped you to feel worthwhile and cared for. As adults in this relationship there should be ample room for him to feel intense love for you at some times, and a playful, lighter affection at others. These affectionate moments cement your friendship, which can endure even when your passionate love for each other takes a brief holiday.

5. Loving Endearments. These are the words of love that you associate with romance, with poets and songwriters, and a full moon on a balmy night. "I love you," "You are my one and only," "There is no one like you." Loving endearments, more than all other forms of positive stroking, express the commitment that he has made to you. These words are special; he means them only for you and no one else. And you hope that the feelings behind these words will last forever. The more special the words, however, the greater the risk.

There are few lovers who have not felt, at some point, betrayed and disappointed after loving endearments have been expressed. Many of my women patients have had trouble getting used to the idea that the same man who is loving one day can be nasty the next. They have a similar difficulty accepting their changes in feeling— from "I love you" one day to "I hate you" the next. Since loving endearments are the language of commitment, it is important that you and your man use these words freely between you all the time and especially after an argument. You not only want to know *that* you are loved, you also want to know why. What is it about you that makes him love you and not another? When he tells you this, you feel more secure, which in turn allows you greater freedom to openly express yourself.

"But she *knows* I love her. She knows I think she's great. I don't have to tell her all the time." No woman has ever been contented with this backhanded compliment, nor has any *man* been satisfied with a lack of praise. Various forms of acting out such as having affairs, working overly long hours (workaholics), and indulging in other kinds of avoidance behavior often indicate that your communications lack appreciation, admiration, praise, affection, and loving endearments. Next we will examine the underlying psychological reasons that he withholds the love that he feels.

Stingy With Love: What Makes Him That Way?

Some partners never seem to be in the same mood at the same time. When one of you is feeling good, the other's feeling bad. Or when one of you is overflowing with tenderness, the other is seeing red. This happens now and then in every relationship, but often, the woman has always been the warmer one. Words of praise and love ripple off your tongue to your man, accompanied by sincere caring. He, however, says "I love you" only on anniversaries and holidays, and his idea of praise and appreciation is to say, when pushed, "Sure, you look nice" and "Yeah, dinner was okay." He is silent most of the times when you need support.

When he withholds love while you exude it, you are involved in an emotional form of unconscious sadomasochism. The withholding partner plays the role of punisher (sadist) while the giver is the one punished (masochist). Some couples play these parts forever. Others may get fed up and switch roles every once in a while, yet the basic sadomasochism continues. This one-up, one-down positioning can be reflected in career success as well. He may be happily successful in his work, while you flounder for direction.

Jacob was the taker (sadist) while Anna was the giver (masochist) until they changed positions. Both in their early forties and married for fifteen years, Jacob and Anna had a perfectly predictable relationship. She was calm, patient, easygoing, and good-natured. No matter what Jacob did or said, she laughed off criticisms and cajoled him out of his depressions. Jacob rarely thanked Anna for this and generally took her support for granted. His work as an architect was exciting for the first few years, but then became a routine that he disliked yet stuck with. Anna, meanwhile, held low-paying jobs as a nurse. Jacob was not especially interested in her career problems, though she listened to his daily litany of woes.

Four years ago Anna went back to school for an advanced degree in health care and has since become a clinic administrator, work she loves and is well paid for. In those years Anna has also had a change of heart about Jacob. She now grows impatient with his constant complaining and is angry at his sullen, withdrawn behavior toward her. She now tells him she doesn't want to hear his problems, and two years ago she told him that she doesn't really love him in the same way anymore and thinks of leaving him. So far she hasn't. Since Anna has become a "bitch," as she described herself, Jacob has steadily improved. He tells her frequently how much he loves her and how great she is and he seems concerned about her feelings. Anna says it's really sad that he's become so nice just when she's stopped being good to him. She can't find that old feeling toward him anymore.

Although it appears that "bad timing" is the culprit here, there is really nothing coincidental about Anna's and Jacob's life together. Their unconscious marriage contract called for one always giving and the other always receiving. Of course, neither of them is consciously aware of this agreement, but they follow it and so sustain this emotional sadomasochism. For the first years Jacob withheld love and support from Anna, the tireless giver who asked nothing for herself. In the past few years their positions have reversed—now Anna withholds from Jacob, who has become the warm nurturer. If the man in your life holds back his love and you are the tireless giver, it is possible for you to alter this pattern once you are aware of the underlying psychological causes.

The first of the causes results from family training. When you grow up without expressions of praise, loving, and appreciation, it is difficult to incorporate them into your adult life. Parents explain their lack of nurturance to their children in a variety of ways that by now have almost become clichés: "You'll get a swelled head if I make too much of a fuss over you," "He never did anything right anyway," "That's just babying the kid—he'll grow up soft." These explanations all sound logical to you as a child and are unquestioned. In Jacob's situation, his father left the family when he was six. Between a rejecting father and an exhausted but controlling mother, Jacob had no loving role model. He learned that his mother became sweeter to him when he was silent and morose, and so he naturally expected that his wife would respond in kind. And Anna was willing to do this because of her own family pattern. Anna's father never spared the rod lest he spoil the child, and her mother was afraid of and dependent on him, as were the children. She treated him more as a king than as a husband. Although Anna's parents were individually proud of Anna and expressed affection to her in words and actions, the model of her parents' relationship—one dominant, aggressive, ungiving partner and one submissive, self-denying but nurturing spouse—was the model that she brought to her own marriage. You can see why it helps to look at not only the way you were treated by your parents, but how they treated each other.

In another situation, Chelsea, forty-two, did not expect Sal, forty-four, to be affectionate or supportive of her—and he wasn't. In trying to analyze why this was so, she realized that her family had been primarily critical instead of loving, and that this had greatly influenced her expectations of men. Not only had her parents allowed her brother to tyrannize her during her childhood, but her mother criticized her father every chance she got, and he barely fought back. Chelsea could not remember witnessing any warm moments between her parents. It's not surprising, then, that Chelsea did not expect any positive thinking from Sal. Once Chelsea became aware of the nurturance she was missing, she began to see Sal's family differently and understood why he didn't appreciate her efforts to be available to him. His mother was a very competent woman who ran the home and also managed the restaurant that she and Sal's father owned. Her husband controlled the profits and spent more on himself than on his family. Sal's father did not appreciate his mother, thus Sal does not express appreciation of Chelsea. Chelsea has begun to discuss the lack of positive stroking with Sal, who is slowly understanding the problem.

Examples of men and women depriving each other of love and nurturance abound in the plays of Anton Chekhov. In one of his most famous works, *The Sea Gull,* a son tries in vain to get attention and praise from his mother, a self-centered actress. In this speech, the son analyzes why his mother does not love him.

You see, my mother does not love me. I should think not! She wants to love, to love, to wear light blouses; and I am twenty-five, and I am a continual reminder that she is no longer young. When I am not there she is only thirty-two, but when I am there she is forty-three, and for that she hates me.

The son here explains that his mother's lack of love is due in part to her insecurity about her age and her attractiveness. Similarly, insecure feelings about himself may cause your man to hold back positive stroking. Feeling insecure about his worth to others as a friend and lover, he hesitates to encourage you to test your abilities—creatively, in business, and interpersonally—because he is certain that if you grow, he will be left behind. Traditionally, women achieved security as the "emotional expert" in the relationship, acting as interpreter between their husbands and their children rather than encouraging the man to fumble in the emotional realms on his own. Men, of course, have held court in the career/business/

money arena, acting as "protector" of the incapable woman instead of supporting her to develop her own skills. Each of you, then, is considered to be superior in one area, inferior in another, and you may feel that the relationship depends on maintaining this balance. Underneath this arrangement lie vast feelings of being unwanted, useless, expendable, and unfulfilled.

You probably know of a situation like Roberta's. For the ten years she was married, her husband, Louis, insisted that only he was to take care of their finances because she would bounce checks ight and left if he gave up control. In finances, he was superior, she was inferior. When their marriage ended and Roberta was forced to handle finances without him, her true skill emerged. Her checks never bounced and she was always in the black. Roberta had definitely felt inferior to Louis when it came to managing money. Unfortunately, his feelings of insecurity stopped him from encouraging Roberta to develop her latent financial abilities. And Roberta had her own agenda—remaining a dependent child. When a man feels insecure, like Louis, he often masks this feeling by criticizing you.

One last example of this is the predicament of Wendy and Victor. Wendy had just started work as a marketing analyst for a large corporation when she and Victor, a medical student, moved in together. Victor was at first very supportive of Wendy in many ways, until she began to earn more money. She noticed that he was now silent where he had been warm, even harsh where he had been kind. Fortunately, she recognized that he had stopped being warm and loving because he felt insecure that he might not be "good enough for her" now that she was successful and he was still struggling. Wendy was thus able to bring up the problem in a sympathetic manner, and Victor did not feel resentful. As upset as you may feel because you are not receiving the support you need, try to assess whether or not his strong insecure feelings are behind his withholding behavior.

Other reasons for holding back warmth come under the category "sibling behavior"; he behaves as if you are his sibling rather than his lover. You may participate in this too. Acting "tit-for-tat"—for instance, saying you won't nurture him if he won't nurture you—is not an effective way of working on the problem although it may help you to feel temporarily relieved of angry feelings toward him. This is, however, what he and his brothers and sisters, or the kids in the playground, did when they wanted to "get back at" someone who had hurt them. Hurt and its companion, anger, are the real reasons that you withhold your love as a way of punishing him for doing the same to you. Competitive feelings and envy—both expressed more often by siblings than by lovers—are, nevertheless, often a part of *your* relationship as well. Competition can motivate you both to excel at something that otherwise you might never try. He's a great skier, so you try to keep up. You garden as a hobby; suddenly he's raising vegetables. For many of us, however, competition has meant that only one can succeed, so others must fail. This kind of competition ceases to be friendly and becomes destructive. He withholds praise because he doesn't want you to do as well, because he hates to share the glory. Like members of rival teams, you and he withhold support, particularly in areas of your own expertise. If you and your man unconsciously play a seesaw game —he is up while you are down, one gives support while the other takes—for any of these reasons, take note.

The last and most important underlying cause for withholding positive stroking is fear. When a man admires, appreciates, praises, and loves you, he feels as if he is emotionally naked before you. "Vulnerable" and "exposed" are words these men may use to describe their conditions. That he may be rejected or abandoned after he has "given his heart" is perhaps the greatest fear. You may have even said, "If only I hadn't told him I care, maybe then he would have stayed." Of course, people who flee from warmth are often experiencing fear. Another reason that he is afraid to express positive feelings is that he fears being absorbed and enveloped by you. He fears that once he praises and admires you, he will somehow lose his autonomy. This is what happened to him at home when he admired his parents or older siblings: They then controlled him. Admiring you does not *have* to mean that he is lessened. In fact, you can tell him that you think more of him because he has the courage to admire a woman.

These fears of rejection and absorption prevented Sylvester from being intimate with Vicki. They have lived together for six years and will, in all probability, eventually marry, though Vicki is angry and discouraged by Sylvester's erratic behavior. Warm and loving one day, rejecting and nasty the next, Sylvester has Vicki never sure what to expect. The owner of a chain of jewelry stores, Sylvester does not seem to know where business stops and love begins. Often, when Vicki approaches him, feeling admiring and warm toward him, Sylvester will greet her "I love you" with words like "Oh, yeah, well what have you done for me lately? Show me and then maybe I'll believe you." At first this threw Vicki into a tailspin; she would feel hurt and examine herself to see what more she could be doing for him. Maybe he was right, she thought. But Vicki eventually figured out that Sylvester was just terrified of her good feelings toward him and this was how he pushed her away. It worked. Vicki became angry and held back her expressions of support toward him to "show him what it was like." Sometimes when he said loving things to her she would use his words, "Show me," then Sylvester would run to find some chores to do to please her. Though Vicki "won," it didn't make her feel any better about herself or about Sylvester.

Vicki's playing "tit-for-tat" hasn't worked, but expressing her feelings of anger and hurt to Sylvester when he pushes her away are a start. She also can try to determine why he reacts like this. Sylvester's mother ordered him around as if he was a servant, and when he occasionally fought back, she told him, "If you love your mother, then you'll do this for me. Now, be mother's good boy and . . ." This type of manipulation conveyed several devastating messages. First, Sylvester learned that he could not love his mother if he did not do her bidding. In fact, she rejected him (i.e., did not love him) unless he did things for her. He also learned that he was not allowed to be himself—to have a different opinion or to be angry with his mother—if he wanted to keep her. In other words, love equals loss of self. His father was rarely at home and then left altogether, increasing Sylvester's dependency on his mother. Not surprisingly, Sylvester acts toward Vicki in the same way that his mother acted toward him: He knows no other type of closeness. Vicki can also identify within herself any similarities to Sylvester. Actually, she can understand that he wants her to prove her love in a practical sense—she only really trusts her friends who have done her favors when she was ill. In this way she and he are alike. She and he will both feel less alienated from each other once she admits that she can see his point (that love equals favors), but that she doesn't want him to use this to stop her from verbally telling him about her loving feelings, and vice versa.

The fear of being hurt also prevents you from proclaiming your warmth and affection. This fear is especially common if you came from a family where a parent is attentive and kind to the child for a while and then, suddenly, becomes harshly critical and punishing. After a time, you become suspicious of loving behavior, and associate love with hurt and pain much the way Pavlov's dogs remembered the electric shocks they got when they touched the wrong door. The shock of a parent's unexpected and unprovoked harshness on the heels of praise and love causes a child to avoid warmth in order to avoid pain.

In another particularly vivid history, Lee spoke about growing up on a farm. As soon as he became attached to an animal—the family dog, a horse, even a rabbit—his father would either give it away or sell it. When Lee protested, his father lectured him about farm animals being work animals and not pets, so Lee stopped having pets. He learned to protect himself by cutting off his loving feelings before they became too strong. As an adult, his girlfriend complained about his lack of affection toward her. By examining his past, Lee could see how defending himself against his father's actions cut him off from loving anyone or anything. He felt angry when he realized that in fact his father got rid of the animals more out of jealousy for the attention Lee gave them than because of some "farm philosophy."

Thus, there are many possible reasons why your man does not express appreciation, admiration, praise, affection, and love to you. Insecurity, family training, confusing you with his siblings, and numerous fears (of rejection, loss of self, and hurt) stop him dead in his tracks or cause him to be silent or even critical instead. The more he resists your attempts to have a warmly supportive relationship, the more active are his fears and insecurities. When you take a risk and ask for more expressions of caring, you may be criticized—told you are "needy," "complaining," "never satisfied," and so on. It will help you to realize that those who withhold love from others are even more needy deep inside their unconscious, and feel so overwhelmed and hopeless about ever receiving what they need that they shut down these feelings entirely. You become the spokesperson for both of you on the topic of positive stroking because you actually are stronger and more optimistic than he. Expressions of love and nurturance on both sides are vital to any relationship, but especially so when you are building a relationship where anger and dissatisfaction can be openly expressed. Warmth and support should never lag far behind anger and should have at least equal time in your communication with each other.

How to Get Him to Nurture You the Way You Nurture Him: A Difficult But Not Impossible Task

Gail Sheehy, in her fascinating book *Pathfinders,* stated that "... people of high well-being usually love mutually. They are rarely involved in relationships in which one exploits for services and the other depends for security, or in which one loves and the other consents to be loved." If you are the one in the position of expressing all the love and providing all the nurturance, and he is the one who "consents" to be loved, then you know how frustrating, painful, and even infuriating it can be. You do not feel like a person of high well-being, but more like a deprived waif who yearns for even a compassionate smile or a tender caress. You need to know how to help your mate to give you verbally the praise (and more) that you need when he is resisting doing this for all the reasons mentioned above.

ROLE MODELING

If you are a supportive, loving mate, you are already role modeling for your man. You may still want to increase your positive stroking repertoire by trying out a technique called fantasizing, or visual imagery. Here's how it works: Try imagining an ideal relationship. In what ways and at what moments would you want the man in this fantasy to be loving or nurturing? For example, perhaps you imagine that the man in your fantasy might say "I love you" for no reason at all, or smile and tell you how important you've been to his life. With that in mind, examine your real life and whether or not you have been treating your man this way and, if not, add this to your communication. Hopefully, he will reciprocate in kind, and you will have made your dream come true by treating him in the manner that you want to be treated. If you are confused as to whether or not you, in fact, are a role model for him, ask yourself, Do I want him to take care of me in the way that I take care of him? If you answered yes, then you are modeling for him the kind of positive stroking that you want in return. If you answered no, then you need to find out why you are withholding. Waiting for him to "be nice first" will not work.

Frequently a woman who is overly nurturing to her man is so either out of habit (she is that way with everyone), starting with her parents—or because she feels that to nurture less means to lose him. You can determine if you are overly supportive by asking yourself these questions: Do I feel used, resentful, even angry toward him after I have been especially helpful? Do I feel as if I am more of a mother to him than a lover and friend? Again, if you answered yes to both, you may be an overgiver. Here are some guidelines to help you determine when to be nurturing:

1. Express love, appreciation, praise, and other positive feelings only when and because you feel this way.

2. Don't compliment (praise, act in a loving manner) to "get him" to love you because you are afraid he has stopped.

3. Don't compliment (praise, act in a loving manner) to get him to do something for you.

4. Don't compliment (praise, act in a loving manner) to "get him in a better mood" if he is upset *with you*. After an argument, however, *do* tell him you love him and care about him if that is the way you feel.

And do tell your man about your love for him whenever, wherever, and as often as you want.

GIVING HIM THE SCRIPT

The second method you can try is script writing, which is essentially telling him what he can say that will make you feel nurtured. This is simple but becomes complicated by his emotional reactions and yours. We will examine your reasons for resisting this method in the next section. There is no more direct and effective way for you to communicate your needs than to tell your man exactly what the words are that you would like to hear. And there is also no method that is more caring than this. When you give him the words to say that will melt your heart, you are demonstrating how much you want to be with him even though he is not the "perfect" man. You are also introducing a value—it is all right to want and need verbal positive stroking, and that it is a sign of strength to acknowledge what you need and to ask for it—that you want to make part of the relationship. Here, then, are some examples of writing the script.

1. You appear dressed and ready to go out for the evening. He does not compliment your appearance. You say, "I'd really like it if you would tell me how nice (pretty, sexy) I look tonight."

2. Once again you've made dinner but he rarely compliments you. During dinner you tell him, "You know I still need to hear that you enjoyed dinner and that you appreciate that I made it."

3. You're having a warm, quiet evening at home. You turn to him and say, "I love you" but he says nothing. You

say, "Would you tell me you love me also? I never get tired of hearing that."

4. Getting your point across at meetings at work has been hard for you. Finally you're able to speak up and the director is impressed. But when you come home and tell your man about this breakthrough, he barely responds. You tell him, "I'd really appreciate it if you would tell me how great you thought I did today at work and how proud you are."

There are many variations of this very direct method, such as asking questions that contain their answers—"Do you love me too?" "Are you proud of how well I did today?" "Don't I look great in this dress?" But use questions like these only if you are sure that he will give the answer you want. If he gives you any reason for doubt, you will be inviting criticism and possibly starting an argument.

TELL HIM WHAT YOU FEEL

By now you may think that he should have gotten the point. And if he hasn't, you probably feel the way the writer Sylvia Ashton Warner did when she said, "God, the illogic! The impossibility of communication in this house. The sheer operation alone of getting something through to somebody." Communication about warm feelings is difficult not so much because you may have a poor asking technique but because of his "hearing" problems, which include defenses against and resistances to intimacy. Because these are often deeply imbedded since childhood, you must be willing to keep trying to bridge the communication gap with alternative responses.

Telling him what you feel—"I feel upset and hurt because you don't tell me how much you appreciate me," or stronger still, "I feel angry because you haven't said one nice word about my promotion," or "I'm disappointed that I compliment you but you don't return the favor"—accomplishes two things. First, it defuses your angry feelings toward him, which have been growing as you give but don't get back, and second, you attempt to break through the wall that he has erected with himself on one side and his loving side and you on the other.

Feelings of anger, hurt, disappointment, upset, sadness, even fury and rage are understandable responses when you don't get what you want, need, and deserve. But many a woman whose man does not compliment her or say he loves her engages instead in cruel mental self-attacks. These women examine their faces, figures, wardrobes, intelligence, and achievements, then determine that he does not love and appreciate them because they are not worth loving and appreciating. This kind of vicious self-criticism not only will cause you endless and pointless pain, but will destroy any hope that your relationship might become more nurturing for you. Attacking yourself because he does not praise you, say he loves you, compliment you, and so on, protects your mate from your angry feelings about his withholding. As long as you criticize yourself, he will not be confronted. More important, though, your relationship will not grow. Many women have asked me, "Isn't it possible that I'm doing something wrong—something to turn him off, and that's why he's not warmer?" Neither you nor your man is "perfect," either in appearance or performance with each other, but your flaws are not the real reason for his lack of expressions of love. His own personal emotional defenses and childhood training are far more powerful in stifling his love. Even if you have been nasty or made a mistake, once you say you're sorry, the incident should be over and neither of you should be holding grudges or withholding love unless you are still living out your childhood problems.

If You Don't Ask, You Don't Get: Why Women Don't Ask for What They Want

Our past affects our present, as we have seen. But the present will also affect the future. John Greenleaf Whittier's famous lines, "For of all sad words of tongue or pen, The saddest are these: 'It might have been,'" are well known to all of us. Why then is it that you are so reluctant today to ask the man in your life for the positive stroking that you know you will want tomorrow? When I have asked my women patients this question, they have adamantly told me why they do not ask their man for positive stroking. These are the most common reasons for not asking, and the deeper psychological explanations behind these reasons.

"I won't ask him because he won't be nice to me anyway. He's just like my father, who never had a kind word but always expected me to look up to him. I would really be angry and resent it if I asked."

Sylvia, who told me this, is actually already quite angry with her husband because he rarely compliments her or says he loves her although he does show her he cares in other ways. Instead of telling her husband what she needs, Sylvia makes sarcastic remarks that thinly disguise her hurt and anger, and do not get her what she wants.

This anger is too intense for Sylvia because it also involves her father, who was too self-centered to give Sylvia admiring attention. Her anger toward him fuels the feelings she has toward her husband. The little girl who was criticized instead of praised felt hopeless about influencing her inadequate father to love her for who she was; she could get his love only by admiring him, and she tried not to act in any way that would cause her to lose it. Feeling disappointed in and complaining about Dad was definitely not allowed. Sylvia is unaware that she is as afraid to lose her husband's approval now as she was fearful of losing her father's love many years ago. Now she projects this hopelessness onto her marriage, and it stops her from trying to influence her husband to be verbally nurturing. In Sylvia's mind her husband is being kind to put up with her sarcasm, but he'd never accept her requests for him to change.

In Sylvia's unconscious mind, husband and father have become one. Sylvia can certainly survive her husband's angry feelings about their problems and will be able to tolerate his angry response to her requests and complaints. But it is even more likely that her husband will listen to her needs, especially if Sylvia feels confident.

"Why should I have to tell him to compliment me? He knew what to say when we first met and I'm sure he hasn't forgotten. No one had to tell my father what to say —he was the most supportive man I ever met." Betrayal, hurt, resentment, and idealization of the male (father) figure are the underlying active components preventing Trisha from helping her boyfriend learn what it is that she wants. A gentle and supportive man to Trisha, her father did seem "perfect" as she was growing up. Trisha's mother seemed to provoke all the fights in the house. Trisha and her father had their special walks and secret looks that said together they could tolerate Mom's explosions. So special was Trisha's relationship with her father that no man she has met since he died measured up. It was easy for her father to be more emotionally intimate and nurturing to her because the anxiety of the intimacy of a real husband-wife relationship was missing. Because Trisha still idealizes her father (in reality he was not an attentive, or understanding, husband), she has not brought together in her mind the real truth that all men have good and bad qualities. She feels so betrayed by her boyfriend, who was much like her father when they first dated but became silent and withholding after they moved in together, that she cannot work on the problem. She does not realize that living together causes unconscious feelings to emerge, and that it is at that point that the real work of a relationship begins. Trisha is also scared that if she does speak up, she will sound like her mother, who always seemed to be screaming, an understandable fear because her mother is her only feminine role model. But once Trisha is aware of these factors, she can find ways not to sound like her mother when she asks for what she wants.

"I'm going to start trouble if I tell him how to nurture me. Either he'll sit there silently and look sad, or he'll be nasty. Whichever it is, I'll get even angrier and the next thing we'll both be yelling. What's that going to accomplish?" Miriam has decided ahead of time what the outcome of any argument or discussion will be. Although her husband is quite stubborn (and may start an argument) her real reason for avoiding any anger is that her father left her mother, which made her mother feel that there was something wrong with her. Miriam is unconsciously identifying with her mother and is worried that her husband will leave her if she asks for what she wants.

Miriam also worries that either her anger or her husband's will escalate into physical violence, something she also saw at home. In reality, because Miriam is avoiding the entire subject of nurturance in her marriage, she is replaying her mother's silent role, living in fear of disrupting the status quo. Robert Louis Stevenson once described a couple, saying, "They have never been in love or in hate." In Miriam's marriage, hate and love need each other. Her husband's silence and withholding behavior have nothing to do with Miriam, but is still thwarting the love he truly feels for her. He is not a violent man —if he does become nasty and angry, he will not hurt her as her father did. Miriam can emotionally survive his anger as long as she firmly believes that she is entitled to positive stroking and that airing this problem between them is a necessary step toward achieving this goal. Although his anger is directed at her, she must be convinced that she is not wrong to want and ask for more verbal expressions of love and caring. Sometimes it's impossible to improve the quality of your life together without "starting trouble." Remember that you are attempting to break lifelong patterns and dislodge old values that said, "We do not say we love each other out loud." "Parents do not have to express appreciation of their children or of each other." "What you do is expected of you." "You do not get praised for who you *are* but for what you do for others." These are loud internal voices that follow you throughout your life and which will require a strong and determined effort to overcome.

Is He Your Everything? Looking Elsewhere for Nurturance

Even the best man in the best of times cannot be everything to a woman. And during the worse of times with a man who is withholding to start, any woman will become deprived if she lacks other support systems. Women who attempt to get enough admiration and praise from one man to make up for the absence of achievements and satisfying relationships outside their love life eventually find frustration and disappointment instead of bliss. Renee's story is an example of this.

Renee was divorced only a year before she met Walter. She had been the one to break up her marriage and had looked forward to the freedom of being single. But when she met Walter, she was determined to make this new relationship work better than her old one had. When Walter asked her to give up the apartment that she had acquired only recently, she was glad to oblige. Walter was supportive of her. He was glad to listen to her work problems, and was frequently complimentary. Renee felt she had found the love she had always wanted. Seeing other friends suddenly seemed a chore, and she stopped taking dance classes and playing tennis because it took her away from Walter. Renee was eager to please Walter, partly because she loved him but also because when he was "in a mood," she felt frantic that he might stop loving her. After a while, when Walter did start to take her for granted and had less time for her, Renee felt depressed and lost. Her only source of self-esteem was gone.

Renee, whose self-esteem had never been very high, was eager to make Walter the center of her life because he made her feel better about herself than anyone else ever did. She had missed out on having parents who adored her and hoped to find this now through Walter. Looking for early nurturance that you did not receive as a child is one of the reasons why you may try to get it all from just one man rather than having several outside support systems going for you. Another reason that you want to forsake everything for him is that you may be afraid not to. This is especially true if you had a possessive, insecure father or mother, who viewed your achievements and other relationships as a threat to their control over you. If they tried to prevent you from having friends or joining a club or the band, you may assume that your man also wants you all to himself. In fact, if he is insecure, he may. You look to him for approval and satisfaction, which he does not give, just as your family required that you stay within their circle for nurturance. The boundaries are never stated outright, but you knew clearly just how close your friendships could be, and how serious your outside interests could get before the family felt threatened.

Ginny, for instance, knew that she could take violin lessons but not join an orchestra. She could take drawing and sculpture lessons but not become good enough to pursue a career in art. She learned of these limits through her mother's depressed expressions and the arguing between her parents, which always seemed to increase if she stayed away from home too much. As a result, Ginny stopped taking violin lessons altogether when she got married, and only occasionally draws. She fears that her husband, like her parents, may withdraw his love if she is successful in these creative areas and receives positive stroking from others.

Erica Jong in her book *Parachutes & Kisses* tells us how her heroine, Isadora, blames her writing achievements for the ruin of her marriage: "She had been good box office since the seventies—but not until her last novel . . . was there anything like *respect* for the way she could write. Did her troubles begin when that newfound success alienated her husband, Josh . . .''

It is possible that your difficult man may feel threatened if you receive admiration and appreciation from other people. But he will probably not tell you that your accomplishments make him feel insecure. Instead, he may show you. Though her husband had never had a drinking problem before, one woman's husband began to drink every evening after she started a small but successful marketing business. What should you do then if your man shows you, or even tells you clearly, that he is unhappy because your interests and talents are getting you positive stroking from outside the relationship? Rather than give up everything for him, which will leave you feeling bitter and stagnant, there are several other steps you can take:

1. Examine your family history to see whether your parents in some manner discouraged you from doing well at what you loved. This will help you to be clear about the differences and similarities between your man and your family.

2. Remind yourself that you are no longer a helpless child who must give up what she wants to avoid being abandoned.

3. Assess what your man says and does to discourage you from leading a full life. Tell him what you observe. Ask him to be more supportive.

4. If he is not aware of what he feels, state out loud what your fears are. Tell him that you are concerned about the impact of your outside interests and success on your relationship. Tell him what you would feel if he were suddenly occupied with a new career or interest. Remain firm on keeping your career or outside interests— you are just airing the feelings.

5. Allot extra time for conversation. Ask him especially about his work and interests, what's troubling him, what's going well.

6. Objectively assess your weekly schedule. Are you away from home more than you are there? Are you using work or other interests to avoid being with him because of feelings you have toward him? Can you adjust your schedule to spend more time with him without giving up what's yours?

"To love is to be engaged is to work is to be interested is to create," said Italian film director Lina Wertmuller. Being alive and fulfilled means that you and the man in your life, like bees collecting honey for the hive, having found your own individual fulfillment, will have more available supplies of affection, praise, admiration, appreciation, and loving endearments to cushion your love through its difficult time.

The Sexual Arena: The Man Who Thinks Sex Is a Chore; The Man Who Thinks Only of Sex

Love had brought her here, to lie beside this young man; love was the key to every good; love lay like a mirage through the golden gates of sex.
—DORIS LESSING

Sex cannot be contained within a definition of physical pleasure, it cannot be understood as merely itself, for it has stood for too long as a symbol of a profound connection between two human beings.
—ELIZABETH JANEWAY

To PARAPHRASE a children's poem, "When sex is good, couples feel very, very good; and when it is bad they feel horrid." When couples first meet or marry, sex is often very, very good. But then, all too frequently, good sex turns to bad sex, or infrequent sex, or none. What was great when you

126

knew each for only a few months has mysteriously changed. You are then flooded by feelings that overwhelm you at night when the two of you get into bed. You are even grateful on those nights when you don't feel like making love anyway, or he doesn't. Because whether you desire more sex or less, more sensitive sex or relief from sex altogether, when the sexual relationship between you and your man breaks down, the anxiety, frustration, anger, sadness, fear, and hurt are as intense as the pleasures and passion when sex is great.

In this chapter we will examine why delicious sex turns sour, and how to take the risk of verbally bringing the problems out in the open. Most of us feel more vulnerable discussing our sexual lives than anything else, as if the essence of our good and bad feelings about ourselves is derived solely from whether or not we are sexually "successful." No wonder, then, that we are so reluctant to say what is wrong. The women I have spoken with, however, have clearly stated two distinctly different sets of sexual complaints. Betty and Dolores exemplify how these two seemingly different problems concerning sex can lead to the same result—the near devastation of a relationship.

Betty is a chic-looking woman who works in the marketing department of a large magazine. Two years ago, while on vacation, she met Zach, who owns a jewelry store. They are both successful in their careers, so money is no problem. Even better, they feel like close friends much of the time, exchanging stories about their daily problems and giving and receiving encouragement. For the first six months after they met, Betty felt as if she were in heaven; she'd finally found a man whom she liked, loved, and lusted after. Zach felt the same toward Betty, and their lovemaking never skipped a day. Yet even before they moved in together a year ago, the frequency of their sex was declining. Concerned, Betty wondered if her mother was right when she said Zach wasn't good enough for her. As the months went on, their sex problem worsened; Zach seemed interested in sex only every few weeks, and whereas he had always seemed to know just what Betty liked in bed, now he would barely touch her before he quickly satisfied himself. Betty's efforts to initiate sex usually led to a fight in which they each would accuse the other of having sexual problems. Worse yet, Zach didn't seem to care about the problem unless Betty became upset, which she was much of the time. Sexually frustrated, despairing, and angry, she thought about having affairs but decided not to. Everything with Zach was so right except for this—but could she live with him and without sex?

Dolores is a terrific athlete. Tennis, golf, and softball occupy much of her time. When she met Phil, who owned sporting goods stores and had played golf professionally for a while, it seemed as if they had known each other a long time. Dolores was soon working with Phil in his stores. She enjoyed their lovemaking when they first met, and Phil also thought it was "great." But after they married, Dolores's sexual appetite decreased; Phil's didn't. He wanted to have sex every day. When Dolores turned him down, which was often, he threatened to see other women or leave her, became cold and silent for hours, and accused her of being frigid. When Dolores had sex more often with Phil to avoid these repercussions, his needs would overwhelm her. Then, when she would turn him down again to avoid having these overwhelming feelings, the fights would start all over again.

Occasionally, Dolores even enjoyed making love, but not enough for Phil. He had always been interested in satisfying Dolores, too, but lately he just wanted her to "take care of him." Usually Dolores obliged, and although it annoyed her, she minded this kind of sex less than the times when Phil expected her to enjoy herself. Their fights ended up being about why she didn't climax, why she didn't like sex. Dolores could not envision a life without Phil yet felt smothered in the relationship during these pressure periods. In the years that they had been married she had twice briefly seen other men—sex with them was easier somehow—but it didn't solve the problem with Phil. She hoped that with their business expanding, Phil would travel more. Maybe his absence would make her heart grow fonder and her sexual interest in him would increase.

Although Dolores and Betty have quite different problems with the men in their lives, both couples are not experiencing mutual passion, the kind of passion that Dr. Otto Kernberg, an eminent psychoanalyst, says should set mature romantic love "apart from all other love relationships in one's life." He adds that passion can provide "an internal wildness that preserves marriage." Betty and Dolores are each more heavily involved in power struggles with their mates than with wildness. Power struggles always develop between a man and a woman when they disagree about how and when to have sex. But these struggles are usually a replay of power struggles that developed during the early years of childhood. For example, Betty's boyfriend, Zach, was an especially compliant, obedient child as a result of having an explosively angry father and overanxious mother. Unconsciously, now, however, any pressure or even requests from Betty trigger in the adult Zach feelings of resentment and anger that he repressed long ago. Although the real battle is between Zach and his past, he and Betty fight each other today in bed. Any power struggle over sex is the result—*not* the cause—of the problem that stops you from having the passionate wildness with your man. The causes lie in the depth of one's unconscious mind, where unacceptable memories and feelings lie forgotten but still remain powerful.

What Else Do You Feel in Bed When You're Not Feeling Passion?

The answer to this question is: a lot, and not all of it is pleasant. Here are the most common feelings that men and women experience to varying degrees while making love.

ANXIETY, ESPECIALLY PERFORMANCE ANXIETY

Your anxiety and his can be caused by a deep fear that you are defying your parents' wishes by engaging in sex, or that you are competing with a jealous parent, who will be angry at you. But another more obvious type of anxiety is about your performance as a sensual and sexual person. Will you both be good enough? What position is the "best" one for intercourse? Will you be able to climax, will he climax too early? Do you need more foreplay than you "should"? What kind of orgasm is best? These are typical of the questions and doubts we all bring with us into the bedroom and that shackle us. Not only his lover, your man thinks of you as one of many critics —teacher, parent, rival sister or brother—just waiting for the opportunity to find his flaws. You and he are especially vulnerable to performance anxiety if you were "good kids" who tried hard to do the right thing or if you are ambitious and perfectionistic in your adult life today. But as you know, the more you try to "get it right," sexually speaking, the less enjoyment you'll derive. People engage in extrarelational affairs to combat strong performance anxiety in order to feel that they are "still good enough." Of course, no number of affairs can overcome serious feelings of inadequacy created by harsh criticisms in early childhood, and affairs can only damage your primary relationship.

DISAPPOINTMENT

This is one feeling few people expect to have after satisfying sex with their partner, yet it wells up in many women and some men. While physically and emotionally fulfilling sex can satisfy some of your wildest dreams, the act of making love may also stir up memories of our past disappointments. In comparison to this joyous moment, those old disappointments make us feel more hurt or angry than ever. Another source of disappointment is described for us by the eminent Karen Horney, who says, "All our . . . wishes, contradictory in their nature . . . are waiting here for their fulfillment. The partner is supposed to be strong, and at the same time, helpless, to dominate us and be dominated by us. . . . He should rape us and be tender . . ." Men also have fantasies of what the perfect sexual partner is like. Although in reality he would not be any more happy with his fantasy than you would be if yours came true, still he may put pressure on you to be more like a particular fantasy of his or be disappointed. But if you understand your own feelings of disappointment, you will feel less criticized. Remember that your feelings of disappointment about your man are connected to all your past disappointments in your life, making the feeling overly intense. Sometimes you are convinced that you two will never enjoy sexual passion together. But that does not have to be the case, if you keep disappointment in perspective.

GUILT

Men suffer from sexual guilt as much if not more than women do. You and he can feel guilty because of your Oedipal desires for your parent, the early childhood sexual attraction to your opposite-sex parent that everyone experiences and most of us resolve in childhood. This is especially common among people whose parents condemned their sexual feelings. In your relationship you unconsciously transform each other into that parent so that what should be normal sex is perceived in your unconscious mind as incestuous sex. In extreme situations, men can feel arousal only with a prostitute or some other "forbidden" woman because their wives or lovers are too firmly entrenched in their minds as Mother, the untouchable. Another kind of guilt occurs whenever you succeed where your parents failed. For example, if you and your man enjoy sex, you can feel guilt about it if your parents did not. You may feel as undeserving of pleasure as they did. Being the third wheel in your parents' relationship—the child for whose sake they stayed together or whose presence is all that made the marriage continue to work—can also lead to guilt.

For example, Sal has felt disinterested in sex since the first year of his marriage to Judith. He's a copywriter, and she's a legal secretary. They don't argue much about sex, but they're unhappy about it all the same. They were married only six months, when Sal's father suddenly died, and since then, Sal's mother has made little effort to get on with her life. Sal feels responsible for her, and Judith thinks that this feeling in some way has contributed to Sal's lack of sexual energy.

Sal feels guilty about his father's death and his mother's dilemma, so he punishes himself by being disinterested in sex. Although he does not know consciously that he feels guilty, he still deprives himself of what is the most pleasurable part of his life as punishment for "causing" his father's death. For some reason, deep down he has concluded that if he had not married Judith, his father would not have died when he did. As illogical as that may sound, in fact, it's possible that Sal's father died when he did precisely because Sal left the family and left him alone with Sal's mother to face the marital problems they had been avoiding for many years. Even if this is true that Sal's father's death does have something to do with Sal leaving his parents for Judith, he still is not "responsible" for the serious problems his parents had had since long before his birth. Obviously, guilt is tricky. You and your man can have performance problems or a lack of interest in sex and not know why. The hidden cause is guilt. Be alert for the source of guilt in your lives when you have sexual difficulties.

EMBARRASSMENT AND SHAME

In Erik Erikson's *Childhood and Society,* he tells us that shame comes about because ". . . one is completely exposed and conscious of being looked at; in one word, self-conscious, one is visible and not ready to be visible . . ." Especially, we could add, when naked or dirty. Feelings of shame are believed to originate during a child's toilet training, when his bowel and bladder control, or lack of it, becomes an issue between the child and his parent. Whether you as a child felt a sense of pride about your new self-control or as if you'd lost a battle for control with your parents will affect if you feel good or shameful about yourself and your body. Shaming experiences also occur at other times that are more easily recollected to most of us than our early toilet training. You may have heard, "What are you doing touching yourself there? That's not a nice thing to do," if your mother saw you as a child experimenting with masturbation. Or as you looked at your naked body in the mirror, you might have been told to "put some clothes on. You should be ashamed of yourself." These comments are spoken routinely with little thought to how they might affect the child's feelings about herself. One woman told me that her mother made up mocking songs about the boys who called her. Another patient remembered that the boys at school taunted her about her early breast development. When she complained to her mother, she was told that she was too sensitive and that they didn't mean anything by it. Unprotected, she felt doubly ashamed still years later.

In another fairly common situation, a young man was kidded by his father about "making it with the girls," even though his father had never talked to him about sex. The son felt simultaneously embarrassed that he didn't seem to know what to do and pressured by his father to perform. Incidents like these, when accumulated over years, create a sense of shame and embarrassment about one's body, sexual feelings, and prowess. You and he carry these feelings into the bedroom, where you unknowingly assume that the other will mock you, poke fun, or be impatient with your inhibitions. A sense of shame can extend to your fantasy life as well, so that you and your man are not free to enjoy your sexual fantasies —alone or together. Children naturally have strong fantasy lives that concern sex, among other topics, but this is often repressed before adolescence.

SADNESS

Although men may also experience this feeling after making love and not express it, I have heard only women describing feeling empty and sad, even crying during and after satisfying sex with their partners. Sexual happiness with a man stirs up unconscious memories of past mistreatment and disappointment. Crying and sadness are an expression of relief and mourning—relief that you are not doomed to be deprived forever, and mourning for the sensitivity and caring you lacked in the past.

Women's complaints that "he just rolls over and goes to sleep" after making love seem age-old and universal. By rolling over, he literally turns his back on all the feelings that he does not want to have—consciously or otherwise—all the feelings that you may be experiencing. Sadness, anxiety about closeness or performance, guilt, even disappointment. It's a confusing assortment, especially if you've enjoyed yourself. Once you accept all these feelings in yourself and understand their past and present origins, you can help your man to accept his feelings too. If you and he do have difficulties with sex, it is even more important to say out loud which of these feelings you think may be stopping the action. Make this a joint declaration. "I think we're both feeling anxious" rather than "you feel anxious." Although your man may be extremely resistant to sexual intimacy and making love altogether at times, it does not mean that deep down he is not "turned on" to you. Rather, feelings from the past and present are inhibiting him. Dr. Mary Jane Sherfey reminds us that "the strength of the drive determines the force required to suppress it." His strong sexual drives may scare him into retreat.

What Can You Do: Taking Emotional Risks for Sex

If you eavesdropped on bedrooms everywhere, you would hear women saying, "Oh, that's all right. It was wonderful for me too. I feel good when you have an orgasm. I really like the cuddling the best anyway." Too often this familiar remark covers up a myriad of feelings and needs that women prefer to keep to themselves, lest they "spoil the moment."

There's no question that sexual discussions do "spoil the moment," and men in particular may complain "Why do we have to talk about it? Why can't we just *do* it?" as if making love were as automatic and intuitive an act as breathing. But, of course, the art of making love is no more intuitive than skiing on one leg. Men and women must teach each other how to please, combining caring and love with sensuality and increasing their skills over time with practice. The status quo between you and your man can be disrupted for a while when you first start to work on the problem, and this prospect scares many women into doing nothing. (Later in this section we will examine other things that may stop you.) But if you are willing to take some risks to improve your sex life, here are some suggestions and warnings.

As we saw in the case of Betty and Dolores at the beginning

of this chapter, there are two distinctly different types of sexually difficult men: the Sex Pusher and the Sex Withholder. What both situations have in common, however, is that the woman's needs are ignored. To deal with either, you must first make it clear to your man that you are not happy. Of course, what you will ask him for after that will differ in each case. No matter which approach is right for you (often the one you design for yourself will be the best), general discussions about sex are more successful when held outside the bedroom during a calm period in your relationship. This lays the groundwork for the specific needs that you will bring up during sex. Here, then, are examples of what Betty (who wants more sex and foreplay) and Dolores (who wants less sexual pressure) might say.

Betty says to her Sexually Withholding Man: "I am upset about what is happening for us in bed. I always enjoyed making love before, but now you rarely have energy, and when you do, you aren't interested in touching me so I enjoy it too. I don't think you're doing this on purpose, but I feel pushed away and frustrated. Would it help if I approached you more, or would you feel pressured? Do you think that work (or anything else) is causing the problem? Should we take more vacations? What do you suggest?"

Dolores says to her man, who is a Sex Pusher: "I am upset about what is happening in bed. I feel pressured by you to have sex when I don't want to and that is turning me off to sex in general. I know you don't mean to do this and I would like us to have a good sex life together. But I need room to figure out how often I like sex and what kinds of touching I need from you. Do you think you can stop coming on to me so often? Perhaps one or two times a week instead? I love you and really want us to figure this out. Do you think sometimes you push me because you are anxious (or angry, or disappointed, or depressed, etc.)?

Both Betty and Dolores are reassuring the man in their lives that they love him even though they are unhappy. They say what they need but they also ask him for help. The questions they ask are designed to raise his awareness about the problem without directly accusing him of causing it. You will find it easier to discuss the problem if you first observe what is best for you and are sensitive to the underlying psychological conflicts. Expecting the problem to be solved after one or two discussions will leave you disappointed. Remember that working through any problem takes time. As the writer Jane Howard tells us, "I think patience is what love is, because how could you love somebody without it?"

As important as they are, discussions outside the bedroom are only half the solution, and the easier one at that. What occurs between the two of you in bed, reminding him of what you want and don't want, is like negotiating an emotional mine field, where your and his insecure feelings lie just waiting to explode with one false step. Men and women tend to "regress" in bed, unwittingly going back to a state of helplessness and insecurity they experienced in childhood. You and he may react to this state by being more passive than usual, more angry, sullen, or withdrawn. Despite these feelings, you must let your man know what you need in bed as well as out. Be gentle but firm and always avoid long discussions. Dolores, for instance, has to remind her husband that she does not want to make love and feel pushed *at the moment* that he approaches her in bed, although she feels scared, angry, and resentful all at the same time. Her husband may become angry, abrupt, and coldly turn away from her, leaving Dolores so upset that she will do anything then to appease him. But she must be confident that in the long run making love only when she *wants* to, and not because she feels she *has* to, will improve their sex life. Dolores can remind her angry husband, Phil, that she loves him and she can even add how much it hurts when he turns his back like that, and that she would like to be affectionate even if they don't have sex. Being affectionate without the pressure of "having sex" is necessary for Dolores but difficult for Phil. It arouses all the fears of intimacy that have been discussed previously. A man (or woman) who is a Sex Pusher is as scared of intimacy in bed as the shy, retiring type.

Betty is also scared to ask for what she wants when she is in bed with her man, a "sex withholder." She is so relieved when Zach is finally interested, she feels she would "spoil everything by criticizing him." If Betty reminds Zach that she wants to be caressed and to climax also (first, perhaps), she is not criticizing but trying to bring sharing and intimacy into their sex life. He, of course, may react as Phil did, with anger and coldness. Betty has an additional fear that not only will this be the end of making love for the evening, but perhaps for weeks. And that Zach will make Betty's "demands" the reason that he has lost interest. If you, like Betty, live with a man who is sexually withholding, it is especially important to remember that his problems originated in his psychological past, not with your requests for attention or foreplay. If you don't keep this fact in mind, you will blame yourself, leaving your man with no reason or incentive to examine his own problems and resistance to sexual intimacy. Blame yourself, and your sex life will never improve.

As a result of her emotional risk taking, Betty and Zach may not make love for weeks. A period of celibacy like this can be productive, for it allows a couple to see each other differently in bed. Generally, your usual sexual patterns must be disturbed for a while if you want him to treat you differently in bed. Women who initiate sex most of the time with a Sex

Withholder will find it helpful to restrain themselves, especially if he rejects you frequently. Examine your own behavior to see if you are being overly aggressive or if you have become a constant complainer (arguments three times a week and more) about the subject of sex. If this is the case, try neither discussing nor initiating sex for a week or two at a time. Complain to your friends or write down your thoughts instead. In the absence of your expressing your feelings, your man may explore his own feelings about making love and about his own needs. Once you are finally in bed together sexually, notice whether you are angry and impatient when you ask for what you need and when you show him how to please you. It is understandable that you would be angry after being deprived, but try not to express it during sex. Explore also whether your feelings have as much to do with your father, who was unavailable or nasty, as they do with your mate. Couples counseling is always useful when there are sexual problems, but it is especially indicated when you cannot stop feeling angry at your mate or when he continues to deprive you, despite all your efforts over a period of time.

Communicating with a difficult man about sex requires more self-confidence than with any other topic. For example, when Zach tells Betty that she "takes too long to climax" and that he loses interest, it will take all Betty's confidence to stop this verbal attack and not blame herself. She must not allow anything Zach says or does to make her question her conviction that mature sex means tenderness and sharing mixed with passion, and that Zach wants this also although he does not show it. Criticizing Betty helps Zach avoid looking at himself. Betty can also remember that there is no "right way" or time limit when they have sex. Zach's unwillingness to caress her for more than a few minutes shows Betty that he is highly anxious about being close, as anxious as she is even though he denies it. If your situation is like this, tell your man about the anxieties you both share and let him know that you need his reassurance that he wants to please you and that he enjoys making love to you, and that you will give him this reassurance in return.

Romantic relationships have the magical power to make grown men and women feel like children again, filled with wonder and awe and optimism about life. Because of this, they provide you the opportunity to get from your mate what you did not receive as a child. But romantic relationships also lead to what Freud called "sexual thralldom," which he defines as "an unusually high degree of dependence and helplessness towards another with whom he (or she) has a sexual relationship. This 'thralldom' can go to great lengths, even to the total loss of independent will and the heaviest sacrifices of personal interests. . . ."

Giving up your own pleasure in bed is certainly a heavy sacrifice of your personal interest, but many women do pay this price because they feel a childhood helplessness in bed that they do not feel in the rest of their lives—the result of "sexual thralldom." Feeling like Daddy's little girl who cannot survive alone, they turn off their needs so that they will "avoid trouble" with the man on whom they feel a "high degree of dependence." The trouble that is being avoided can take many forms. In Sheila's case, brutal rejection in the past and a difficult man in the present combined to frighten her into silence in bed.

Sheila was working in the sales department of a large insurance company when she met Ted, a vice-president in another department, at the office Christmas party. The chemistry between them was so strong that within a short time, Sheila left her boyfriend, Ted left his girlfriend, and she moved into Ted's place. Sheila had never been very assertive sexually, so she was at first pleased that Ted always made the overtures. But after a while, she began to feel that his needs were more like demands. Half the time what he wanted was to be satisfied by Sheila through oral sex. At other times, he was a sensitive lover. If Sheila ever turned him down, Ted threatened to see other women or to pack her bags for her and change the locks, which made Sheila afraid to say no. The few times they'd had these fights Ted had not actually make good on any of his threats but Sheila still panicked at the thought of making him angry. She wanted to stay with him but she wasn't sure if this was because of her fear of being alone or because she loved him. It was probably both.

Sheila is in "sexual thralldom" with Ted. She thinks she cannot manage without him. His threats take her back to her childhood in which she felt terrified of her father's temper. He had hit her brother when he got angry and once made sexual overtures to Sheila, which she ran away from. When Sheila feels too frightened to tell Ted no (that she is not there to be a sexual servant), it is because she has made Ted into her father, and herself into a helpless little girl. In fact, Ted is not violent, and she is not helpless. Once she understands this, Sheila can then tell Ted that he is not to threaten her when he is angry but should express himself directly. Deep down, she knows that Ted is not going to carry out his threats (although her father did). She also knows that if Ted did, she would not want to stay with him anyway and that she would survive without him. And, despite his bullying, Ted shares some of

142

Sheila's fears. Underneath his bravado, Ted feels he cannot survive without sex with a woman (without Sheila, because his mother was quite controlling and made him feel he could not survive without her). Once Ted is forced to do without sex occasionally because Sheila is strong enough to say no, he will realize gradually that he does not need it to survive. Their lovemaking can then be for pleasure rather than as a means of coping with their mutual fear of losing the other.

Another reason that Sheila does not ask for what she needs sexually is because she fears anger—hers, Ted's and her father's. When Ted's "eyes bulge and he gets red in the face," Sheila is paralyzed. "I hate it when Ted is furious like that. I feel all alone and without a friend in the world" is the way she describes herself then. Since Ted gets very angry when Sheila says no to him, you can understand her hesitation to provoke him. One thing that would help Sheila is doing a few mental exercises to increase her courage and confidence.

1. She can remember what it was like to be a little girl with an angry, sometimes violent father. She can remind herself that she is not the small child now and that Ted is not her father.

2. She can realize that she does have friends and is not alone in the world.

3. She can recall past incidents when Ted has been angry and nothing terrible happened.

4. She can remind herself that anger lasts only a brief time and passes.

5. She can know that Ted needs her as much as she needs him, and that Ted is also afraid of his own anger and should learn to express himself in a more productive

way. As Sheila becomes less afraid of him, he will be forced to do this.

Jealousy—the Unavoidable By-Product of Sex

Jealousy is the feeling you get when you perceive another person as your rival for someone else's love. A three-year-old feels it when Mommy pays attention to the new baby, and a twenty-four-year-old may feel this when her boss praises someone else rather than her. As a twelve-year-old, you very likely felt jealous when your "crush" of the moment gave a big smile to the girl in the next row.

Jealousy and love are like Siamese twins attached at the heart—they go everywhere together and one can't live without the other. The presence of sex only intensifies jealousy. Edmond Rostand equates love and jealousy when he wrote, "Yes, that is love—the wind of terrible and jealous beauty, blowing over me—that dark fire, that music . . ." Since, according to Freud, desiring the parent of the opposite sex is a universal phenomenon, then jealousy, of course, is also universal and part of the human experience. Even when we know this to be true, most of us are repulsed by our jealous feelings. We consider jealousy a spoiler more damaging and frightening than even anger. We believe that if others see us as being jealous, we will be humiliated and made to feel vulnerable. So instead of feeling jealousy, we seek to avoid it. We may try to defeat jealousy by being overly nice to a woman of whom we feel jealous, or we may use loads of makeup and exercise seven days a week in order to "win" our man from a rival. Your man may withdraw into a shell when he is jealous or angry. But there is no way to eliminate jealousy entirely unless you live alone on a desert island. Trying to deny jealous feelings often has the same effect as continually avoiding anger. There's either an explosion of long pent-up feelings or a complete emotional withdrawal from the relationship. By the time that happens, nothing of the relationship can be salvaged. Once again, you have to take the lead by teaching your mate that jealousy is okay, bearing in mind that he is more afraid of it than you are.

How you manage your jealous feelings as an adult primarily depends on how your parents handled this feeling when you were a child. For example, Rita's mother often had angry spells that lasted for days. As a child, Rita assumed that something she had done caused it, though, as she learned many years later, the real target of her mother's anger were her father's frequent extramarital affairs. Her mother denied that they existed, and so her jealousy and anger took the form of "spells" over unimportant issues around the house and anger toward Rita. Eventually, Rita grew to believe she could never please her mother; her parents' marriage ended. In her adult relationships with men, Rita was insecure, eager to please, and kept her jealous feelings to herself as her mother had. As a result, she was often mistreated.

Rita's mother thought jealousy was "wrong." But jealousy is natural and necessary. Mothers feel jealous of daughters and daughters of mothers. Fathers feel jealous of their sons, and so on. Fathers and daughters are often distant because of Mom's unconscious jealousy. A father and daughter may forego having a close relationship in order to keep Mother happy. Too often, fathers are overly critical and competitive with their sons about careers, intelligence, and capabilities, when the underlying issue is really jealousy of the son's closeness to his mother. You and your man, then, feel insecure and learned that jealousy is not something you talk about, though everyone knows it's there. But what can you do then when you live with a man who makes you feel jealous and on edge all the time?

Veronica and Lionel have had an uneasy three years of marriage. In the first few months Lionel had eyes only for Veronica. But since then, he gawks at other women—on the street, in restaurants, even the wives of the couples that they see socially. His blatant stares embarrass Veronica, but Lionel seems not to care. In his job as the manager of a computer store, Lionel surely meets many women, and Veronica is not always sure she trusts him, especially when she sees how easily he appears attracted to them. At his office parties Veronica always feels that one or two of the women are giving her icy stares. Is it because they have designs on Lionel? He denies that he was eyeing their mutual friend's wife at dinner, and that he has a special friendship with a woman at work. Each time Veronica feels jealous, she confronts Lionel. His angry response—that she must be crazy—makes her even more suspicious. Why would he get so upset if he had nothing to hide? Veronica also yells during these exchanges and cross-examines Lionel as if he were on trial. She inevitably ends up crying.

Even if Lionel is telling the truth, at the very least, he *is* a flirt. This does not make Veronica feel good when she's with him or secure in their relationship, which is Lionel's unconscious plan. Like his father, Lionel feels especially anxious in social situations. Unconsciously, he flirts with women to ease his anxiety and to get reassurance that she cares enough to be jealous. He is never sure if she, or any woman, cares enough. When Veronica gets upset he knows she cares. His relationship with his mother was just like this.

But Veronica does not know any of this because she is too upset to be objective. When Lionel flirts, he plays to her unconscious fear that she will never be able to keep a man. Her father took her mother's side against her in their frequent arguments. Yet, when Mom was not around, Dad made her feel as if she were the most important woman in his life. Veronica seesaws between feeling like Father's wife and like a family outcast. Lionel's behavior makes her feel the same way.

Though Veronica could not communicate with her father about this problem, she must express herself to Lionel. Cross-examining him doesn't help; in fact, Lionel feels right at home being criticized, since it smacks of the kind of negative attention he got from his father. Realizing that Lionel feels as insecure about her as she does about him can ease Veronica's fears. Perhaps now she can put into words her feelings and needs to Lionel instead of criticizing him. She might say "I know you're not doing this on purpose, but you're getting me jealous and angry when you're eyeing other women. It hurts me so badly that I hate you at that moment. I don't even enjoy going out anymore together. I want us to feel secure about each other, but how can I feel secure when you're looking at other women?"

In this speech, or a variation of it that suits you, Veronica is direct about what she feels and what the problem is. After this, there are numerous possible solutions open to her depending on the amount of cooperation she gets from Lionel. Let's assume that Lionel responds angrily and says "You're crazy if you think I was looking at anybody. You need a psychiatrist" and leaves the room. If your man reacts like this, do not pursue him at the moment. After he calms down, bring up the topic again. This time you can try working on a solution. First ask, "Do you want to help me to feel better when we're out together? Because if you do, I have some suggestions." If he is still uncooperative, tell him what you feel and reflect back to him how difficult he's being. "I feel disappointed when you act like this. What am I supposed to do when you walk away from the problems? Are you telling me to look for someone else?" You may bring up your feelings about his flirtatiousness each time it occurs for months before he is willing to help solve the problem. How long this process will take depends on the kinds of problems in his family background and how insecure he feels about you. When he is ready to cooperate, here are some suggestions as to what to ask for that will help you to feel better.

1. In general, when you are out together, ask him to pay more attention to you, smile at you, be attentive, tell you he loves you.

2. Agree on a secret signal or code phrase that you can give him when you feel that he is being overly attentive to another woman and ignoring you.

3. Tell him that at these moments it will help if he would put his arm around you, hold your hand, or give you a hug.

This kind of reassurance will allow you both to enjoy being with others yet still feel secure in your relationship. When he feels more secure, he will not need to flirt with other women so intensely and ignore you. If you are suspicious that he is actually seeing other women, ask him about this directly. You will feel better if you both restate your commitment to monogamy. As always, seek professional help if you two cannot resolve the difficult jealousy issue together.

Jealous feelings are certainly among the most painful, but in expressing these feelings you and he tell each other how valuable you are to each other in a way that can't be duplicated. You give each other a precious gift. Although these feelings may seem unmanageable at first, when you have made each other feel secure, jealousy in its milder, less destructive forms becomes an expression of love. Without love, there is no jealousy. Without jealousy, there is no love. As Minna Antrim wrote in 1902, "The 'green-eyed Monster' causes much woe, but the *absence* of this ugly serpent argues the presence of a corpse whose name is Eros (Greek god of love)."

Touchy Topics: Vacations, Gifts, Money, Divorce, Marriage... He Never Gets It Right

Life was a labyrinth of petty turns and there was no Ariadne who held the clue.

—RUTH BENEDICT

It was hard to communicate with you. You were always communicating with yourself. The line was busy.

—JEAN KERR

THIS is a common occurrence. Two couples are out for the evening, having a pleasant dinner, when the conversation turns to the upcoming holiday. Suddenly one of the men angrily says, "We have to go to *her* crazy family again." His wife glares at him, but for the sake of having a peaceful evening, says nothing. Though the other couple quickly changes the topic, everyone knows that an explosive scene has narrowly been avoided, though certainly not forgotten.

Every couple has their own list of these "hot spots" much like the Pentagon's map of troubled areas of the world. In between these hot areas, all is relatively calm, and workable solutions can always be found. But whenever they cross the border into a "hot spot," blood pressure jumps, voices are raised, and muscles tense. No matter what the specific problem may be, you and he become instantly embroiled every time the topic comes up. You are both so emotionally charged about the issue that you are convinced no workable solution is possible. "Touchy topics" can at first remain isolated from the rest of your relationship. But over a long period of time the one unresolved issue can contaminate the rest of your life together. As Willy Loman told us in *Death of a Salesman,* "Attention must be paid." Even when we know in our rational moments that the problem must be and should be resolved, it is still difficult to concentrate objectively on an emotionally charged subject because the feelings rush past you in a blur. You don't want to fight about it again, but in a flash you two are arguing about where you will spend the holidays, and how awful his family—or your family—is. Your feelings are as intense as if you never discussed it before, when in fact you've been at each other about this at least ten times.

This kind of dispute follows a pattern, and learning to observe the chain of events can help you cope. These are the five key points:

1. Which one of you provokes the other into the fight, which quickly escalates?

2. How long do your arguments last?

3. How do they end?

4. Do the fights take place at a specific time of the day, with or without others around?

5. Does one of you win these fights? Is it you or him?

With this information, you can see and change your role in the fighting ritual. A man who is otherwise reasonable can become impossible about one subject over and over again. When the subject comes up he loses all sensitivity and ability to communicate. Men who are difficult easily feel controlled, whether or not you are trying to control them. Thus, in this chapter, I will present ways to approach common problem topics so that he will less likely plant his heels and you can more likely negotiate what you want. In addition to stepping back to observe the fight ritual, you will need to know what are the underlying psychological issues for him and for you on each topic. Once you know this, you are well prepared to resolve the problem.

Unfortunately, when you are angry with him for the tenth —or hundredth—time about the same issue you don't usually step back from the timeworn argument long enough to decipher the underlying messages in the communication. Even if deciphering the emotional "code" will not resolve the problem instantly, if he feels understood (and you do too), he will feel more like compromising on the issue that started it all— holidays, money, family, or even marriage. Lurking behind every real-life here-and-now hot spot are deeper feelings and needs that are more meaningful to you both. Let's take a careful look at several of the more common concrete issues that tend to become touchy topics for couples and their deeper underlying emotional conflicts. Your and his underlying feelings will differ somewhat depending on your family history, but you will see how to take a potential crisis situation, turn it inside out to find the real problem, and then use it to grow closer to your mate and enhance the relationship. What we often regard as the petty issues that make up day-to-day life are never really petty.

Financial Feuding

Money may not be the "root of all evil," but it is the subject of a lot of arguments between couples. Finances seem to be woven into so many of our casual social conversations—what to buy and how much will it cost, how to make money and where to invest it, the lack of money, and finally our fantasies about hitting it big someday. When we talk so much about money, what are we really talking about? More important, when you fight about money, what are you really arguing about?

Our concepts of money, basic dependency needs, and power are interwoven from the day we were born. As a child your daily requirements of food, clothing, and shelter are provided by your parents, who held the purse strings. If you were sent to bed without dinner (a cruel punishment) you could not take yourself to the nearest restaurant or grocery store to make up for this deprivation. Whether you grew up with only the barest necessities or in the lap of luxury depended on your family's financial status and their attitude about spending their money on you. You looked to your parents for financial and emotional support. Perhaps they were the only ones to turn to. Thus, those who had the money had much power—to provide for you or not in terms of love and money. In many homes, money substitutes for emotional closeness; discussions about finances replace discussions about feelings. Your father, who you wanted dearly to appreciate you and to be interested in you, may have shown his interest only through giving, or taking away, money. Because of childhood conditioning, you may think that you need someone who has more money than you do to take care of you. You might even feel that you can't take care of yourself without this other person—thus giving power and control to whoever holds the purse.

Money is the only thing Beth and Walter fight about, and they fight about it a lot. After living together for two years, Beth and Walter are very much in love. She works for a record company, where she met Walter, an aspiring musician. Music is their mutual passion and they go to concerts as often as they can. The problem seems to be erratic income; one month he works a lot and money is no problem, but the next two months he may not work at all. Beth's regular paycheck carries them through Walter's dry periods, but she is furious about this and criticizes Walter constantly because she feels he could be doing a lot more to help them out. He insists that he needs to be available in case someone calls him about a music job and he needs the free time to practice. Beth feels awful when she thinks about breaking up with Walter, but she doesn't know how she could have a child, which she wants, with someone like him, though she does think he would make a great father.

Though they fight about money, the real issue here is who is going to take care of whom. Each of them wants to be taken care of by the other in the same way that their parents took care of them. In both cases, their parents supplied money in lieu of emotional nurturance and used money to keep them dependent. Beth and Walter are much better at giving each other emotional support than their parents ever were, but since they have unconsciously made each other into parental figures, they still yearn for the old familiar kind of parenting that's connected with money. When they are feeling stronger about themselves, they also want to be successful and financially independent. Thus, when Walter resists getting a part-time job to tide him over, he is unconsciously telling Beth that he wants her to do what his parents did—support him. At the same time, Walter is also afraid to make more money because deep down he thinks that his success would make Beth feel unhappy and insecure. He has Beth confused with his father, who certainly would feel threatened by his son's success. And Beth has Walter confused with *her* father, who felt he had nothing to give Beth if she were financially solvent. Uncovering the deeper issues—in this case, wanting to remain dependent on your partner the way your parents kept you dependent on them—will help Beth to work out compromises with Walter. Telling him that she has discovered that they share these deeper conflicts can help to bring them closer. Instead of fighting about money, they can be allies in helping each other deal with their mutual problem.

Couples also fight about money even when there is enough. They may start frequent arguments by criticizing each other's spending habits or behaving secretively about their finances. Donald, for instance, criticizes Lynn about any purchase she makes without consulting him. Lynn fights back by justifying the expenditure, no matter how small. They have been feuding this way over her spending for ten years. But what they are really fighting about is not money, but control. And fear is the feeling that makes us need control. Donald feels safe only when he is in control, and Lynn feels safe only when she is controlled. But there is a healthier part of each of them that longs to break out of this arrangement. Although Lynn may not be ready to give up this mutual control pact, she can begin to investigate her past and Donald's for the roots of their fighting.

Coming from a poor family where money was the number one topic, it is surprising that Donald doesn't dwell on it even more than he does. His criticisms of her spending are just attempts to re-create the same type of conversation they had in his home. Knowing this, Lynn would see that his criticisms of her had nothing to do with *her* financial abilities. For her part, Lynn, meanwhile, is used to being criticized by her mother and, to a certain degree, doubts herself. Both having lived with controlling parents, she and Donald are scared to live without them. Here, then, is a way for each of them to see how similar they are on a deep feeling level; they both want someone to be controlling their money and they both want to fight about money. Once you can see how similar you are and stop blaming each other, you are halfway along to solving the problem.

One last money-related problem occurs when he is so obsessed with making money that he ignores your relationship. He seems to be, as Hilaire Belloc wrote ". . . tired of Love . . . But Money gives (him) Pleasure all the time." A woman fights with her man because she feels she's been neglected and abandoned for that elusive mistress, money, or the job. Sometimes the woman may even blame and criticize herself, thinking that she has not been "interesting" enough or done enough to keep him at home. At other times, she will verbally attack her mate or demand that he be home at a specific time. Sometimes this works to solve the problem, but often it does not. It can help, though, to know that your money-obsessed man may be scared of many things, such as being intimate and close to you. He is probably also scared of the angry and loving feelings he might have toward you if he spent more time with you. Quite likely he is scared, too, of losing his identity, or merging, with you, whereas at work, he is always clear about who he is. Perhaps because of his background he lives in constant fear of the wolf at the door even though he has left poverty far behind. Underneath your anger and hurt about being rejected, you are also scared—scared that the love and fun have gone from your relationship and that you are being ignored. Try to get him to spend time with you but let him plan what you will do together. Again, it is easier to work out this solution or any other once you know that underneath the conflict you share a fear. In this case, he fears merging, you fear not merging.

Vacation: For Pleasure or Pain?

There are as many opinions about the value of vacations as there are people who take them. Some feel that vacations are a necessity. Others see taking a vacation as indulging in a luxury that they cannot afford, or are not entitled to. Still a further cause for divisiveness is the question of whether you desire rest and relaxation, enduring an adventure/survival experience, or soaking up a centuries-old culture. When you consider the multitude of choices, you can see why this is a frequent hot topic for couples.

Rose and Oscar argue all year long about whether or not to take a vacation. In the seven years they've lived together, there's been more talk about vacations than you'd hear in a travel agency. Rose's opinion is that she cannot survive without at least one two-week vacation away from everything each year. She avidly collects brochures and describes these fantasy vacations to Oscar. Oscar's feeling about vacations is that they cost a lot of money, then they're over, and what do you have left to show for it except a couple of pictures. He'd rather spend the money on a new television. As the years progress, these fights don't change much. Each sticks to his or her point of view. Rose gets very upset, cries, and sometimes they take the vacation she wants, but then she wonders if it's worth all the trouble. Oscar usually ends up having a better time than she does anyway.

As in Rose and Oscar's case, the vacation is rarely enjoyable for both of you. Either one of you feels resentful, gypped, or anxious to get back to work or just anxious in general. A vacation like this doesn't bring you two closer or provide the refreshing break from your daily routine. Of course, everyone has very specific ideas about how to spend their free time, but when these discussions result in arguments that recur for years and sabotage your vacation pleasure, or you end up vacationing alone or separately, it is crucial that you recognize the underlying psychological forces that hold you at this impasse.

Oscar's parents had never traveled farther from home than a four-hour drive could take them. When Rose whispered to him of Hawaii or Paris, he felt guilty. If his parents couldn't have these wonderful trips, how did he deserve them? When Rose understands this, she will find the same feeling in herself, for she also feels undeserving of vacations. In fact, when she approaches Oscar, she acts as if she is asking his permission, not telling him what she wants and deserves. Here, then, is a feeling they both share, despite the fact that each expresses it differently. Even if Oscar doesn't want to understand this about himself, he will not want to be left behind when he accepts that Rose has decided not to continue feeling "undeserving."

One reason that you may fight about vacations is because going away means that the two of you will be alone together for an extended period. Just as this situation offers infinite possibilities for intimacy, it can also cause anxiety. Your man may be anxious because he could be "found out" on a vacation —have exposed those parts of his personality that he feels are unattractive to others. Shirley Jackson, a writer, described this well in her book *Raising Demons.* "It has long been my belief that in terms of great stress, such as a four-day vacation, the thin veneer of family unity wears off almost at once, and we are revealed in our true personalities." Although Ms. Jackson writes humorously, what she is saying is true. Fortunately, many couples on vacation find that their true personalities are far more sexual and relaxed than usual, and that's one reason many people seem to literally live for their vacations. But those who are too anxious and stressed tend to argue more. You can break this cycle if you and your man can both agree that, for whatever reasons, vacations make you both feel insecure and anxious, and that this common enough feeling should not stop you from taking care of yourselves. Understand and reassure each other when you travel. Perfectionists may have a difficult time with vacations because they expect that all will be picture-postcard-perfect—an impossibility in any part of the real world. Some couples hope to have "perfect sex," an expectation that raises anxiety and dampens excitement.

You and your man may argue about vacations because deep down you feel undeserving of or guilty about accepting this treat. People whose parents did not like it when they were away from home may experience this. Their parents longed to keep them home as much as possible. One woman I know rarely took vacations. The first few times she did, one of her parents fell ill a week before her planned departure. Although she was determined to allow herself her vacation, she had to contend with a lot of guilt and anxiety and make frequent calls home.

Gift Giving: A Delicate Subject

O. Henry wrote a beautiful but sad short story about gift giving in which a newly married couple try to give each other special Christmas gifts. Since neither has any money, each secretly sells their only treasure in order to buy the other a gift; the man sells his heirloom watch, the woman her long precious locks to a wigmaker. Alas, they open the gifts—a gold watch fob for him, beautiful combs for her—only to find that neither has any use for them.

Anyone can "make mistakes" when giving gifts, even the most well-intentioned. Common problems between men and women in relationships are often due to the man "making a mistake." He either forgets the event for which the gift was expected, or buys something that upsets his mate for no apparent reason. The forgotten gift or card, the present that was not at all what you expected after dropping hints for a month, cause feelings of hurt and anger that will reverberate through the year if allowed to do so.

Tania, for instance, felt her love for Maurice waver in the first year of their marriage because of the gift problem. A physician's assistant for several years, she has been thinking recently of attending medical school. Though her feelings rarely trouble her, recently she's felt very emotional since Maurice forgot their first Valentine's Day together. She still feels uncared about, is silent around him, and cries a lot, which makes Maurice angry. Worse yet, for Tania's birthday Maurice gave her a necklace that had belonged to his mother for years because he knew that Tania liked antique jewelry. But Tania was shocked to see that the piece, though pretty, was a cheap costume item. Tania felt that Maurice had just wanted to save himself some time and money. Tania feels her love has been shaken, and Maurice is disgusted with the whole business. He swears he'll never get her another present.

Tania's and Maurice's concerns about gift giving run deeper and involve more than just choosing the right memento. For one thing, these feelings are interfering in the resolution of this problem. For women especially, gift problems can symbolize the imminent end of their Prince Charming fantasy about their man. Suddenly you feel that you cannot or don't want to trust him with your love because he might hurt you like this again. Even though he is attentive to you in many other ways, you shut out his warmth because of the thoughtlessness of the gift. Often women who feel this strongly previously idealized men, beginning with their fathers. They see their fathers (and their mates) as flawless, so they are shocked and crestfallen when the fantasy ends. An inferior gift (or none at all) also can symbolize the deprivation of love and acceptance from one or both parents. In this context, the gift problem just seems to prove that no one ever takes the time to figure out what it is that you want and need.

For a man (or woman) who forgets occasions that he knows are important to his mate or does not try to work out a way to find out what the right gift would be, other unconscious forces are at work. "Forgetting" or giving the decidedly wrong gift can be an expression of unconscious hostility. In this mild form of acting out, he tells you—without revealing anything directly—that he is upset about something. This secret anger usually stems from an authority problem; he feels pushed around and controlled about many things, one of which is having to buy gifts. This feeling originated in his childhood and now he perpetuates it with your help. As much as you try to get him to give you the gift you want, he may try just as hard not to. But another of his possible underlying feelings has nothing to do with control. The man in your life is probably having trouble keeping the different women in his life clear in his unconscious mind. You, his mother, his sister, his ex-wife or girlfriend may all be merged in his mind so that he really can't figure out how your specific taste, for example, differs from theirs. Perhaps his mother never appreciated the gifts he gave her, so now he feels inadequate to the task. Another reason why he may not be doing what you want is that you may be asking him to change his family tradition. His family may not have exchanged gifts at all or placed very little importance or emotional value on gift giving.

Working out a compromise solution on gift giving is not difficult once you stop feeling like enemies and understand where his feelings and yours come from. Have a discussion before the event, where you both decide whether or not you'll exchange gifts and specifically tell the other what you want, and you will eliminate many problems. Going together to pick

162

out expensive gifts is another good method. I have talked to women who resent giving instructions like this to their mates. They complain that these solutions take the fun, surprise, and romance out of the ceremony. Similarly, men complain that the women are criticizing their taste and don't trust them to purchase the right gift. Putting up this type of resistance to solving the problem should make you two feel closer than ever, since it comes from wanting to be understood, appreciated, and "have your mind read" by the other without having to say or do anything. Both of you resent communicating verbally. Hopefully, the closeness you feel about this will smooth the way to an easier exchange of gifts.

Love Me, Love My Family: Family Fireworks

No single topic arouses as much passionate arguing and good-natured joking as the family. Mother-in-law and brother-in-law jokes are part of our culture. But so is family violence. The Canadian writer Mavis Gallant tells us that "no people are ever as divided as those of the same blood . . ." while Jill Ruckelshaus, active in government, says, "The family is the building block for whatever solidarity there is in society." If knowledgeable opinion differs this radically, it is not surprising that you and the man in your life have strongly different feelings about each other's families and even about how involved you want to be in your extended-family life. This was one of the topics for argument between Maude and Patrick.

Though Patrick and Maude both work in the stock market, they retain a wholesome look that betrays their country roots. Both of their families live across the country, so it is surprising that they argue so much about them. Recently Patrick's sister Sally has moved near them, and Patrick speaks to her almost every day on the phone. Maude began to feel that she and Patrick cannot make a decision without Patrick consulting his sister. She blew up when Patrick called Sally to ask what movie she and Patrick should see. Patrick defends his relationship with his sister in these fights by saying that Maude is just jealous and that his sister knows more than Maude about certain things, like movies. Patrick tells Maude that Sally is a better listener than she is and more sympathetic. Maude of course feels insulted and furious, and she hates Sally more than ever, especially since Patrick used to praise her the same way.

This couple is fighting about family loyalty and much more. Without realizing it, Maude and Patrick are using a defense mechanism called "splitting." In splitting, a person attributes to one individual all good qualities while attributing to another person all bad qualities. Here, Patrick has made his sister the "good" one and Maude the "bad" one. Like any defense mechanism, splitting helps Patrick to feel safe and protected with one person at a time because he sees only that person's generous, caring qualities. He ignores any characteristics that might cause him anger and upset his positive feelings toward Sally. When he is with Maude, the reverse occurs. Patrick can keep himself from experiencing anxiety about his intimacy with Maude by ignoring the warm feelings between them.

On her side, Maude feels deeply jealous and possessive of Patrick whenever his family is around or even mentioned in conversation. Maude acts antagonistic because she feels left out and is scared of being rejected. She is very much like Patrick in that she thinks, unconsciously, that you can feel loving toward only one person at a time; someone *has* to be the odd woman out. If Maude can step back from the problem, she will see this similarity. She will also realize that Sally looks up to Patrick the way that Maude used to when she was younger and in the infatuation stage of love. Patrick is indirectly stating his anger toward Maude about this change through his sister. Maude can then try and talk to Patrick about what she observes. She might say, "I'd rather you tell me directly about your feelings toward me instead of using Sally to get at me. When you play us against each other it damages my friendship with her." She can also tell Patrick how they both split people into camps of the "good" and the "bad," and how she hopes they can be a team together. With her self-understanding and understanding of their mutual problems, Maude has a good chance of resolving this problem with Patrick.

Sue and Jeff are another couple who argue about family matters. Most recently the problem arose because Jeff's parents wanted to take a vacation to Hawaii with them. Sue was convinced that a vacation with Jeff's parents would be no vacation at all. Jeff partially agreed with her but felt powerless to say no to them. Sue told him that he was "no man at all" if he couldn't stand up to his parents. Sue might have tried to understand that Jeff was feeling dependent on his parents as if he were a child again. He yearns for their approval and love because he is scared of losing what he needs to survive. Sue is not understanding Jeff because she denies this strong need for approval within herself. When she scorns Jeff's childish behavior with his parents, she is also scorning the dependent child within herself. Their first step to solving this problem is to recognize their feelings of dependence on their parents. Sue could be sympathetic but maintain her position about separate vacations. This would give Jeff the support he needs to have his own life with her. They might even rehearse Jeff's conversation with his parents or propose some alternative to a vacation, such as spending a weekend with them instead.

One last reason why you and he argue about your families is the psychological concept of "merging," which is best explained through an example.

Ted and Melinda go to visit Ted's folks a few times a year in the small New Hampshire town where he grew up. Melinda notices that once Ted walks through his parents' front door, a country drawl replaces his city accent, and for the next two days he barely notices her until she complains loudly. Ted is merging with his parents, being temporarily absorbed back into the family unit, and reassuming the old role he played when he lived there. The lines that define his sense of self—which are not always very clear even when he's with Melinda—disappear altogether during these visits. In the town where he grew up, being "separate" and "different" was considered wrong —almost sinful—and so, unconsciously, Ted is afraid to be himself with his parents. Ted was always "different" from his family, which is why he moved to a big city. Although on the surface his parents seem proud of his success as a salesman with a large insurance company, his achievements set him apart and they have never really accepted him as one of the family. Ted desperately wants this acceptance, and so he automatically merges with his parents when he visits them. Part of this merging requires that Ted camouflage who he is to prevent his parents' criticism or mistrust of "that city feller," which would be painful to him and make him angry.

Melinda, knowing that she is witnessing a merger, can be relieved by the knowledge that this condition is temporary and will cease when they return home. But while Melinda is being understanding, she should also make her feelings known to Ted, both because she will feel better and it will help to shake him out of his childlike state. Ted may get angry with Melinda when she points out that he is ignoring her and that she wants to be included. This, of course, is the misdirected anger that Ted really feels toward his family for not accepting him with his differences, but once he has "let off steam," he will probably be able to define himself better with his parents and pay more attention to Melinda. Wanting to merge into a symbiotic unit with your family is a feeling we all have no matter how far you've moved or how separate your life is. When you and your man acknowledge that you both have this desire, you will be better equipped to stop merging into the past and stay instead in the present with each other.

The Holidays: Cutting through
the Emotional Traffic

When Bing Crosby sang that he was "dreaming of a white Christmas just like the ones [he] used to know," he indelibly stamped in our minds the vision of the perfect Christmas. In reality, though, the holidays more often than not fall far short of fulfilling this vision. Couples frequently fight about holidays —who they'll spend them with, where they'll spend them, and how they'll celebrate. Whether it's New Year's, Thanksgiving, or a long Memorial Day weekend, holidays can be fodder for many years of unhappy discussions.

Francine and Claude have been unable to resolve their holiday problem in their eight years of marriage. Instead of enjoying the preparations and festivities for Thanksgiving and Christmas, they argue about whose family they will be with. Each wants only to be with his or her own family and resents any time spent with the in-laws. Although they have tried various solutions—alternating holidays between the families, inviting both families to their home (a disaster, since neither family was happy and Francine was overwhelmed by all the work)—nothing they've tried allayed the difficult feelings both have.

As with the other "touchy topics," when the obvious reasonable solution doesn't work and the fight continues, underlying psychological conflicts are holding you back. First and foremost of these is the conflict between your holiday fantasies and reality. When you idealize how the perfect family would spend the perfect Christmas, you fall into the same kind of trap we discussed before regarding the so-called "perfect couple." The fantasy may soothe you temporarily with the hope that this year your dream will come true. But here again, the fantasy provides only a convenient, temporary, and flimsy escape from your daily problems. You may expect that the holiday will make up for long-standing feelings of deprivation—perhaps on this one special day "something good will happen to you for a change." Unfortunately, the more you idealize a situation, the less likely you are to be satisfied with whatever does happen. Francine and Claude, in part, argue with and blame each other for making the holidays miserable so that they avoid seeing two crucial points: their imperfect families are imperfect on holidays, too, and nothing ever happens on a holiday that can cure your recent or lifelong feelings of dissatisfaction. As long as they can understand they share these feelings, they can feel a rich sense of intimacy that will make up for the absence of "the perfect holiday."

Guilt also ruins many celebrations and can spark fights between the two of you. If you and your man feel that you are responsible for making other people happy before yourselves, then you will be torn between doing what is best for your relationship and what is best for others.

Esther loved to go out to dine and dance on New Year's Eve. Her fiancé, Bob, wants only to stay home and watch TV. His reasons sound logical and convincing, but, in fact, none of them really has anything to do with his steadfast refusal to budge from their apartment. From the time he was a child, his mother had suffered from crippling arthritis, and he could not remember a New Year's Eve that she had enjoyed. His guilt about having a better time than his mother was having tied him in a not that kept him from planning an evening with Esther that would make both of them happy.

Being able to compromise and plan your holidays together is symbolic of building a solid family life together. As long as you see each other as rivals for holiday plans, you will feel like frustrated children competing for an ultimately unsatisfying prize. But if you can understand the conflicts you have in common, you will experience a fascinating and warm sense of intimacy, no matter what plan you make.

The Divorce Doldrums: Becalmed in the Past

When you and he are together, but one or both of you procrastinates about divorcing your ex, it's like having a shiny new car that's missing an engine—no matter how great it looks, it's just not going anywhere. The arguments that you and he have regularly about this problem don't get anyone moving either. Charlene and Greg have lived together for five years, and the fact that he still hasn't divorced his wife after years of separation is a problem.

Charlene knew when she met Greg that he was married though he hadn't lived with his wife for two years. Charlene was right to assume that Greg was not going back to his wife, but she seriously underestimated the time it would take him to get his divorce. She believed it would be only a short time before Greg was divorced, and his promises to Charlene sustained her fantasy. After two years of living together, Charlene became skeptical and began to complain more strongly than before. She discovered that Greg, a well-off doctor, had not signed even a separation agreement for what he termed "financial reasons" although he had been supporting his eight-year-old daughter all along. Every time Charlene raises the subject, Greg promises to get the divorce soon—he just has to wait until his ex-wife finished school; six months later, he was saying he had to wait again so he wouldn't "lose his shirt" to her. Charlene's now angry and she worries that if she did ever marry Greg he would procrastinate about everything.

A divorce is often hard to get—not for the reasons Greg offers—but because of the unconscious feelings we all have about separations. Divorce ranks among the ten most traumatic life experiences, right up there with the death of a spouse, a job change, and moving. All of these can cause severe emotional and physical stress, and also, understandably, many people postpone indefinitely taking the final step. Greg's fear of being abandoned is largely responsible for his lack of action on his divorce. He is insecure about whether or not Charlene will really marry him once he is "free." Despite the fact that Greg had not lived with his wife for years, he still unconsciously feels that he "has her" (and she, him) because they are legally married, and this connection, as weak as it is, prevents Greg from feeling the terror of being alone. Charlene, meanwhile, unaware of Greg's fear, waits for him to prove his love to her by getting a divorce. Greg, of course, is waiting for Charlene to demonstrate her undying devotion to him so that he can feel secure enough to finalize his divorce. Charlene can communicate more effectively with Greg and break this deadlock when she is aware of the psychological conflicts, like fear of abandonment, that paralyze him.

Another obstacle for Greg is transference. His wife, especially because she is the mother of his child, represents, unconsciously, to him his own mother. He feels guilty that he will no longer be taking care of her and because he is, symbolically with this divorce, leaving "Mother" for another woman, Charlene. He worries that he cannot survive without a woman who needed him as much as his wife did. These feelings do not occur only in men. If you, the woman, have been postponing getting your divorce, you are probably having similar deep conflicts about whether or not you can survive without your husband, at least partially because he represents your father to you. You also are susceptible to feeling guilty about leaving your "father" for another man. You feel like a child with your husband. From my experience with many couples, the transference phenomena is especially strong in first marriages, possibly because these couples married at an earlier age, and so were more likely to think of each other as parental figures.

Jean Kerr in her play, *Mary, Mary,* had this to say about divorces: "Well, being divorced is like being hit by a Mack truck. If you live through it, you start looking very carefully to the right and to the left." People who are getting or who have been divorced start looking around very carefully for fear of making another mistake, having another failure. To many of us, divorce represents personal failure, and so your man may be postponing his divorce to put off making a mistake or feeling like a failure. And, unconsciously, he may know that being "free" increases the chances that he may make another mistake, something he is safe from while he's still married. The more you can identify in yourself all the feelings that the man in your life might be experiencing about his divorce proceedings, the more supportive you can be to him. You can explain to him what you feel is really happening in this situation and add that you would feel the same way if you were in his position. You are less likely to feel personally rejected and will be better able to discuss this with him without getting into a power struggle or name-calling battle or withdrawing altogether. As always, though, understanding him does not mean negating your own feelings. Telling him clearly what you feel, what you want, and that these delays are detrimental to the future of your intimacy together is equally important. He needs to know that you are serious about your future together and that you want him to be too.

Marriage: Cold Feet Can Mean Hot Arguments

The seventeenth-century writer William Congreve said about marriage: "Courtship (is) to marriage, as a very witty prologue to a very dull play." Such a dismal assessment of this institution would prompt anyone contemplating marriage to have at least second thoughts, if not cold feet. Sadly, many people agree with the pessimistic Mr. Congreve. Anxiety and fear of a dull future without fun and passion is one of the reasons that the man in your life may have cold feet about marriage. When you *want* to marry and he is skeptical at best, dead set against it at worst, the subject of tying the knot becomes explosive. Even when you both agree that you will marry in the future, anxiety about the actual event can still precipitate arguments, tension, and fear. There are many feelings about marriage that run deep, and their sources run deeper still. That things will go from good to bad, as Mr. Congreve puts it, is one of the arguments your man may give as the reason for saying no.

May and Ned, who've lived together three years, start out discussing marriage and end up arguing. It's only in the last six months or so that either of them thought at all about marriage. Many of their initial problems, which started on moving-in day, have been worked out and so marriage seemed like a natural step. When May brought it up, Ned's reaction was mixed. He could see it as a possibility for the future but thought it would cause difficulties that so far they'd avoided, such as disagreements about money. "You'll probably think you can tell me what to do with my money if we got married," he told May. May was hurt and angry because Ned's money was the last thing she thought about. Since they were both teachers and each earned about the same salary, they'd always divided expenses evenly. Still, a few weeks later, Ned brought up marriage. This time May was cautious. She told Ned that she was now worried that he might start having affairs once he was an "old married man," though this had never been a problem while they lived together. Now Ned was hurt and angry.

Ned and May are looking at marriage through their parents' experience of it. In Ned's family, money had always been a problem, and when his parents broke up when he was a teenager, he saw money as the reason. May saw her father as a big flirt, whom she suspected of fooling around. Although her parents are still together, her mother still seems jealous when other women are around her father. But, as is usually the case, this is not the whole story. May and Ned also give each other some reason to have their individual worries. May wants to have a baby and stay home for a while while Ned pays the bills, and Ned has, in the past, been flirtatious, which has upset May. Despite these things, neither has given the other sufficient reason to be as pessimistic as they are about their future together. It will be helpful for you and your mate to be aware of your particular fantasy of how things may go wrong and where this fantasy comes from so that, like May and Ned, you can determine how much of your problem is in the present and between you two and how much comes from history. Concentrate on solving the present problems as they are rather than as you envision they will be later.

"If we have problems, should we get married?" is a question many people ask. Your man may be worried and afraid that if you do marry, your problems will grow and worsen and he will be trapped forever in a bad marriage. This thought inspires panic in him. There are, however, many other underlying causes for his panic which are not caused by your problems together. Will his friends, his children, his parents approve of this marriage? Will he "become" like his father? Will his mother be able to manage sharing him with you? Discuss with him these possible other sources for his anxiety. You might also consider premarital therapy to gain insight and find solutions together to the old problems that suddenly seem so pressing.

As you can see, in "touchy topics," there is always "more than meets the eye." Unearthing these deeper, unconscious thoughts and feelings may seem exhausting at first and will stop you at times from having spontaneous outbursts of your feelings toward your difficult man as you spend time, instead, looking for the "real" causes of your fights. The positive aspect of this is that you will "think first and act later," always an advantageous course to follow in any emotional encounter. One last point. It is best to ask your difficult man "Do you want to hear what I think is really going on here for us?" before you tell him about the underlying conflicts and feelings. Try not to ask this in the heat of a fight. After things cool down will be soon enough. Even if he continually "stonewalls" your efforts, *you* will still benefit by feeling more in control of yourself and more objective in these mini-crises because you understand the origin of the deadlock. If, despite your best efforts, the hot spot remains an especially sore area in your relationship over a period of time, couples counseling would be indicated. More likely, though, you both will grasp the chance to be understood and to understand each other's underlying feelings—creating a climate for compromise and, ultimately, a loving relationship.

Time for Self-Evaluation: Are You an Overcomplainer or Silent Sufferer? Seven Communication Traps to Avoid

Self-expression must pass into communication for its fulfillment.
—PEARL S. BUCK

We have to face the fact that either all of us are going to die together or we are going to learn to live together, and if we are to live together, we have to talk.

—ELEANOR ROOSEVELT

To BE proclaimed a "shrew" by the men around her is every woman's nightmare. Kate, Shakespeare's famous heroine in *The Taming of the Shrew,* was feared and disliked because of her sharp tongue. The one who finally dared to pursue her did so only because of her rich dowry. Will it be your misfortune to be called a shrew and a nag if you state how you feel and what you want? A large number of women, whom I will call the "sufferers," hold everything in (at least in part) for fear of appearing shrewish. Unhappy, angry, feeling mistreated, these women choose not to say anything at all except on those rare occasions when they "can't hold it in any longer." Gloria lived her life that way.

Gloria, a lanky redhead who works as a commercial artist and model, had a child four years ago. She and Nick have been pretty happy during the eight years they've been married. They're both proud of the fact that they rarely, if ever, fight. Gloria admits, however, that she found it easier to take things as they came *before* she had a child. Now, running from the job to the nursery school and home, where the housework awaits, she rarely has time for herself. She needs personal time, but she so hates the idea of quarreling with Nick about his lack of initiative in housework and child care that she avoids the subject. Instead, she finds herself making sarcastic comments or criticizing him about really insignificant things. Nick acts as if he doesn't notice there's anything wrong. Gloria has decided that maybe nothing will ever make her happy, so why talk to Nick about the problem? You can sympathize with Gloria's plight and understand her reluctance to provoke or allow any conflict to upset her already complicated life. But her silent martyrdom is slowly eroding the warmth that she feels for Nick.

Like many of us, Gloria has a list of reasons why she does not want to bring up touchy subjects.

1. She does not want to be "upset all the time." Gloria is sure that once she opens up the gate holding in her feelings, she'll never close it. She wouldn't mind saying words without all the feelings that follow, but as the French writer Colette told us, "All those beautiful sentiments I've uttered have made me feel genuinely upset." Feelings do follow words.

2. Gloria assumes that "if I have to change him, then I shouldn't be with him." She thinks that she should accept him the way he is, for better or worse. After all, he believes that he is doing the best he can. Gloria thinks he has a right to his opinion, even if she doesn't like the results.

3. Anger, and plenty of it, is the third reason that Gloria does not want to confront Nick about her feelings and needs. Whenever Gloria thinks about feeling dissatisfied and emotionally abandoned, her next thought is that she must leave Nick immediately. In these moments she tells herself that he will never give her what she wants and she is wasting her time with him. Her anger toward Nick is so strong that Gloria is certain their relationship would not last if she expressed it. In Gloria's mind it would be better to get out than to try opening up to Nick and risk his rejection.

Many women underestimate their man's ability and willingness to face conflict and change. Before they even attempt to communicate, these women have convinced themselves that he is inflexible and will "turn them off," reject them, or even leave them. As long as there is pleasure in a relationship, most men not only will tolerate but welcome the opportunity to become more emotionally intimate. When Gloria complains

179

that she doesn't want to "change him," she means that she thinks Nick really isn't capable of being more emotionally expressive and involved in their life together. If this is true, then the job she faces is impossible. However, most of us were born with the natural ability to convey all our emotions—and with the desire to be giving in a loving relationship.

Of course these innate abilities may have been blocked or somehow made weak by years of unexpressed anger, jealousy, and fear. To understand this better, it helps to know the therapeutic term, "ego." The ego is the inner part of ourselves that negotiates the environment for us, evaluating our internal perceptions and memories and planning a course of action between these and the outside world. Most of us have had our otherwise healthy egos battered and bruised over the years by a variety of influences. Fortunately, no matter how injured one's ego is, it always retains the capability to change. When you communicate your feelings and needs and then permit your man to do the same, you are appealing to his healthier ego. You cannot force him to change, but you can influence and reach out to the healthy parts of the ego. Every "silent sufferer" has her reasons for being that way, which are more likely to have come from her childhood past than from the adult present. In my work with couples and with women in relationships, I have rarely seen any two people who are "untouchable," that is, unwilling and unable to connect with each other in a more productive way. Before you give up on him and retreat to suffer in silence, assess your reasons, examining your own past as well as his. If your father was unreachable and your mother never tried, it still doesn't mean you and he are like them. If you operate under blanket assumptions and foregone conclusions, you are surely underestimating yourself and him.

Much more likely than the sufferers to meet the fate of Shakespeare's "shrewish" Kate are the "constant complainers." Silent women are unable to start talking; complaining women can't stop. Though their complaints are usually justified, the frequency and duration of their grievances hamper them in getting what they say they want. Josephine realized one day that she had become this complaining type.

A computer analyst, Josephine looked like a no-nonsense type woman, though her short cropped straight hair and dangling earrings gave her an exotic aura. For four years it seemed that she and her husband, Stan, had argued every single day. Josephine admitted that she instigated all the fights, but Stan's passive behavior at home and his shutting her out of conversations around others just drove her wild. His passivity extended to the bedroom, where she was fed up with being the aggressor. His occasional overdrinking was another sore point. Still, she loved him and he loved her, though some days all she did was yell and nag at him. She couldn't seem to help herself or stop from saying things like "You never do anything around here and I can't stand it. You're just a taker and I'm sick of being the giver. You don't even try to make me feel good about myself as a woman. Sometimes I think it would be easier if you didn't make it home one night when you've been drinking. I'd have an easier time as a widow."

Stan's responses to Josephine's verbal attacks vary. Sometimes he just looks bewildered and hurt and grows more quiet. But more often he yells back, insulting Josephine, calling her

181

a "pushy bitch—a controlling princess who just wants to run my life." Josephine not only loudly criticizes Stan daily, but often does so for an hour or more. Occasionally Stan has even shaken her to shut her up; once or twice he's walked out. Josephine's nagging approach doesn't work because it places her on Stan's merry-go-round. Since he was a child, Stan has been gliding through life, never having to address any serious emotional problem directly, while every woman in his life—from his mother to Josephine—yells at him.

Besides criticizing Stan too often and "going on and on about everything," Josephine does not tell him how she feels (though it's obvious she's angry, hurt, frustrated, and scared of the future with him) and what he needs to do to make her happy—either a change in his behavior, or giving him the words to say that will make her feel better, at least temporarily. Another thing she may want to work toward with him is seeking out some kind of counseling together. But none of this can occur in these destructive confrontations, or afterward. This couple is locked into an old struggle. If you are a constant complainer like Josephine, knowing the underlying reasons why you "can't stop" may help you to be more understanding of yourself, and hopefully feel more in control of what you say. Let's look at these causes.

We all need to feel emotionally connected to other people in order to live. Studies have shown that infants who are not held will not eat, and a sense of well-being that enables us to function comes only from lifelong contact with others. One reason why you may be a constant complainer with a man who is withholding and passive is to fill the void of silence that would otherwise envelop you. Author Germaine Greer described this silent condition when she said, "Loneliness is never more cruel than when it is felt in close propinquity with someone who has ceased to communicate." The woman who talks obsessively about unresolved problems is afraid of this loneliness. Usually, she was raised in a home where arguing was a constant—perhaps even the only—form of communication. Any lapse in the constant din reminded the family members how separate they really felt from one another and how terrified they were of that. Without the know-how and courage to relate to one another warmly, they fell into substituting their loud, passionate arguments for meaningful communication. You can see how someone from this kind of family would prefer complaining and nagging to silence. When Josephine's talking stopped, she felt all alone in the world. Stan's family did not know how to communicate their feelings, so they fought off the dreaded silence with newsy chatter. There might have been an occasional nasty explosion from his father, which the family dealt with by burying it in more chatter. More often than not, when Josephine stops talking—whether she's complaining or not—Stan is silent. He finds it as difficult to warm up to conversation as Josephine finds it is to cool down.

Another reason why you are talking "at" him too frequently is to avoid painful feelings. Words seem to dispel or allay the intensity of your feelings toward him. The frustration, fury, anxiety, sadness, and hopeless feelings that may threaten to overwhelm you when you are alone or with your silent man are not as acute when you are talking. How unfair it all seems—you feel everything, while he seems to feel nothing. You are yelling and upset, and he seems to be counting the seconds until you'll finally stop. He thinks your complaining all the time is the only problem in the relationship. But things are rarely what they seem, and neither side's story tells the whole truth. Passive, apparently unfeeling people sit and wait for the other guy to express their feelings for them. The hidden contract in your relationship with your seemingly stonefaced mate is that you are his emotional mouthpiece. What upsets you about him upsets *him* about him too. The problem is that he can't, or won't, admit that, at least not to you, because you represent a parental figure to him. Subconsciously, he wants you to harangue him—either because he was yelled at like this by his parents, or because your yelling at him gives him more attention than he ever got at home, or for any one of many other reasons based in his past. When couples act out opposite emotional roles with each other, their situation is called complementarity. (It will be discussed more fully in a later chapter.) Because you two are playing out old roles, you must slow down and change your communication tactics.

Do a Family Evaluation

Although you cannot control your man, you can influence him. The only control any of us really can exert is over ourselves. When you step back and evaluate your family, you take a step forward in gaining control over yourself. In the following situation, Abe is driving Chloe up the wall. But she can gain some control over herself if she will evaluate her family and identify the common threads running between her past and present.

The thing about Abe that got to Chloe was when he came home late. If he called to say he'd be late, then he'd be home even later than that time and she would be left twiddling her thumbs, growing impatient, and finally working herself into a fit. Eventually, if he was fifteen minutes late to meet her and their friends at a restaurant, her evening would be ruined until she could get home and let him have it verbally. At this point, Abe was ready to let her have it physically, and it was after a mild hitting match that Chloe realized things were out of control. Why was she letting Abe's lateness ruin her life?

Before Chloe could evaluate whether her family and Abe had anything in common for her (and whether this pressure from the past was pushing her out of control in the present), she drew up a list of how Abe made her feel. She felt rejected, that he didn't care about her, and that anything or anyone else meant more to him than she did. His lateness also made her feel that he didn't really want to be with her. As she thought about these feelings, Chloe began recalling things from her past. Her father had always been too busy to spend time with her. Whenever he was around, her mother would grab him away for some special project or outing. The terrible frustration and hopelessness Chloe felt toward Abe was a replay of the feelings she had about ever being special and close to her father. This hopelessness had contaminated all of her relationships with men. As a child she had not felt that her father cared about her, but she did know today that Abe loved her and wanted to be with her; he had shown that in many ways. His lateness, though upsetting, wasn't an expression of a lack of love. As constant complainers often do, when Chloe complained vehemently she was expressing anger and frustration not only about the present, but also about the past. As children, few of us have the opportunity or the words to say what

185

we feel to the parent who has hurt us. But as adults, we gain the courage and the words, and we use them with the man who we know will stay around.

Chloe's obsession with Abe's lateness has as much to do with her father's avoiding her as it has to do with Abe. Once Chloe understood this about herself, she concentrated on Abe. He was obsessed with being late, and he refused to live any other way, it seemed. Chloe could tell that his very sense of himself—even of his masculinity—seemed connected to his chronic tardiness. She knew it had nothing to do with her and that Abe would have to deal with this problem on his own when he was ready. Chloe's decision to change how she communicated with Abe (which, briefly, means bringing up her feelings less and attempting to keep her intense anger and anxiety away from their talks) came about because her old way of doing things was not good for *her.* Self-interest is the best motivation for doing an emotional overhaul. Any change you make will be more effective if you are convinced that it is for your benefit, not his.

We will now see how you can evaluate where on the scale between suffering and constant complaining you belong, whether you should raise or lower the volume of your communication, and how to change the content.

Determining Your TQ (Talk Quotient)

Evaluating yourself is difficult, because you can be harsher, more critical, and more demanding of yourself than anyone else would be. Thus, in order to assess your talk quotient— how often or how little you criticize and complain—you must banish from your idea of yourself those concepts of good and bad, right and wrong that we all carry with us. In the world of relationships, except in the case of physical violations, there is no right or wrong, no good or bad. Self-understanding and self-awareness are the only principles that you need as you assess how you relate to the man in your life.

Are you a silent sufferer or a constant complainer? As you read the following descriptions of each type of woman (men fall into these categories too), if at least three of the characteristics describe you, you may want to change your way of communication.

THE CONSTANT COMPLAINER

1. You are "at him" verbally every day, sometimes several times a day about his "problem areas."

2. You can hear yourself get louder and more agitated as he gets quieter while you talk "at him."

3. You tend to run to fifteen-minute monologues (or longer) as you pursue him from room to room.

4. You feel worse, more anxious, or depressed—even out of breath and physically exhausted—by the time the verbal joust or monologue is over.

5. You do not feel that all your talking and fighting with him is productive for you or him over the *long term*. You always feel as if all your talk is a waste of energy. You think about leaving him but mainly feel frustrated.

1. You bring up your feelings in a confrontational way, maybe once a month, maybe less, maybe never.

2. When you do speak up, it's not planned and it may not make sense—it's an explosion.

3. You make and keep a mental list of what he has done to you, but you rarely tell him.

4. You often feel as if you want to explode but rarely do so.

5. You feel as if you and he are moving further apart emotionally.

6. You do not feel that these very infrequent fights or discussions are productive in the long run. Immediately afterward you are determined *never* to bring up anything again. Then you feel that you ought to leave him.

The constant complainer and the silent sufferer have much more in common than it may appear. For starters, neither one is taking any emotional risks. They do not want to leave themselves open to feeling vulnerable, which is what will happen if they say how they feel and what they want. In each case, the man is working hard to protect the status quo, unhappy as that is. Both are miserable and feel trapped in their old roles. Complainers and sufferers both fear what will happen to themselves and their relationship if they "renegotiate" their unwritten contract. The worst fear, of course, is that the relationship will end. Although this is always possible, it is much more likely that things will improve, not deteriorate, if a complainer talks less or a sufferer talks more.

Your communication pattern or style has three different components that you must change if you want to improve your relationship: the quantity of talk, the content, and the quality of your voice or emotions when you speak. Chloe agreed to a one-day-a-week moratorium on all complaints about Abe's lateness, no matter what Abe did that day. The moratorium was gradually extended so that Chloe mentioned the problem less and less. Chloe told Abe what she had observed about the way they got along and let him know that she was going to try to stop pursuing him. It is important to tell the man in your life what you are doing and why, whether or not he agrees with what you're doing or thinks it will work. Even men who are "antipsychology" appreciate being included and that you are making an attempt to improve the relationship. Once Abe no longer felt "hounded" by Chloe, he was free of the power struggle and could accept how destructive his lateness was without feeling that he was "giving in" to "pushy Chloe."

Some last comments about quantity. Drastic changes will not feel good to either of you, but gradual modifications will. If you two rarely discuss issues, try once a week calmly bringing up a problem instead of exploding on impulse. You can cut down in the same way. Since romantic relations are about as orderly as a house after a New Year's Eve party, these alterations in the frequency of discussions will never be as organized as you might wish. Whenever you are unsure about how often to discuss your feelings, remember that too much talk is safer for the long-term health of your relationship than too little. There is no way to improve how you and he communicate unless you two practice, and there is a good chance that even if you have not understood each other, airing your feelings may clear the way for closeness again. Holding it all in increases the emotional pressure, and the inevitable explosion might be so messy that no one would want to clean up.

What you say is as important as how you say it. Remember, state your feelings first, then follow with the specifics of your complaint. Asking for what you want is the third part. If the man in your life has his head in the sand about his own feelings, you may add what you think *he* feels. However, be careful not to analyze his problems out of anger; it will only make him feel that he's being attacked. And if you are extremely angry, wait until you feel calmer before you ask for what you want. You will not be a perfect communicator from the beginning, so don't punish yourself or retreat into silence if your first attempts go awry. After all, you and he can always say "I'm sorry," and keep trying.

Develop an Early Detection System

If you and he have frequent verbal battles, where you both "lose," observe how these fights start. What are the early warning signals? A woman told me that she could tell by the way her husband's lips were pressed tightly together that a fight was imminent if she mentioned her feelings. By reading his signals, she learned to stop the argument before it spiraled out of control. Instead, she waited until they had both cooled down before she told him what she needed from him.

Although we might agree with the writer Cynthia Ozick when she said, "In saying what is obvious, never choose cunning. Yelling works better," speaking *with* your emotions but without yelling works better still. Screaming, yelling, cursing, and name-calling have really only one benefit—what therapists call "ventilation." You air out the stale, bitter feelings that have been smoldering in the dark and clear your emotional passages for new feelings, thoughts, and experiences. This process may be necessary for you to maintain your day-to-day well-being and that of the relationship. For this reason, ventilating is preferable to silence, especially if he ventilates too. But saying everything uncensored and uncut, as loud and as long and as angrily as you want, will not encourage emotional growth. Besides, getting what you want from the man in your life by yelling at him can become a habit for both of you. He may stop giving you what you need without being screamed at, and that is *not* a step forward. Ventilating your feelings loudly should be used sparingly and with discretion. It cannot substitute for actual communication. If you cannot talk to your man about problems without raising your voice, then you are carrying an overload of anger that needs to be dumped somewhere else—by talking to a therapist or a friend, writing down your most vicious thoughts about him, or by fantasizing conversations that you would love to have with him but won't. Conversely, you may discover that you sound apologetic and weak when you say "Maybe we have a problem here and could you possibly please try to . . ." This response indicates that you do not trust your feelings and could use the help of a friend or therapist for support. Since a difficult man does not make it any easier for you to express yourself, you will need other people to give you that important confidence.

How you talk—too much or too little, too loudly or too weakly, too critically or too apologetically—is much less important than making sure that you *do* communicate and not let your feelings pile up. You may find that you must let him know how much he upsets you the instant he does it, or you may choose to wait until the following day. The best way to tell how frequently to let out your anger is to measure the warmth you feel toward him. When you cannot measure any loving or warm feelings toward him, it is time to open the floodgates and let your anger escape so that there's room for warmth. Now that you are communicating, we will examine some common pitfalls on the road to emotional intimacy.

Seven Communication Traps to Avoid

The battlefields of relationships are littered with the exhausted emotional remains of women who fought the good fight trying to get their man to respond to their feelings. They repeatedly fell into traps that were either set for them or of their own making. Here are the seven most common communication traps.

1. Criticizing his loved ones, making angry demands

2. Having all-night "discussions"

3. Needing to be right

4. Power struggles

5. Holding grudges

6. Guilt

7. Falling for his diversions

Knowing what the traps are and where they are set can help you to avoid them.

Trap #1: Criticizing His Loved Ones, Making Angry Demands

Wendy was frustrated over her inability to get her husband, Mike, to understand how she feels toward his mother. She thought that Mike let his mother get away with meddling in and controlling their every move. Usually what she says runs along these lines: "I can't stand the way your mother wants to be involved in everything around here. And her opinions are always wrong. She doesn't want to let go of you, and it's driving me crazy. Are you going to stand up to her when she calls the next time or not?" Wendy thinks that after she says this, she has expressed—and he should understand—exactly how she feels. But, in fact, the message isn't getting through.

When Wendy says these things, she stumbles into several traps that may be familiar to you. First, she tells Mike her negative feelings toward his mother. It is *never* productive to tell your man negative feelings you have toward his family, his friends, even his dog. Telling him how you feel about *them* is not the same as telling him how you feel about *him,* though talking about people close to him is often a "disguised" discussion about him. Second, Wendy criticizes Mike's mother, whom he will naturally defend, whether he agrees with Wendy or not. Criticizing and listing the faults of his family and friends to him is rarely helpful except in cases where he expresses himself first and needs you to concur. A communication like this, that has little to do with feelings, creates animosity and will not get you what you want. Third, Wendy asks Mike for something (to stand up to his mother) in the heat of anger, so Mike hears her request as a demand. Angry demands always meet resistance because they draw us into power struggles. (Power struggles are another trap which will be discussed later in this chapter.)

In her speech, Wendy neglects to mention her most important feelings—the ones she has for Mike, probably because Mike means so much to her. She deals with her fear of saying what she feels toward Mike by talking about his mother instead. She is afraid to ask Mike to stand up to his mother when she is not angry because if he rejects her, then she will not have her anger to protect her. She also hates bringing up unpleasant subjects when they are feeling good together because she's sure it will spoil their good time.

But Wendy is also tired of rehashing the same subjects without anything ever being resolved. She is ready to try something new. Here's what she might quietly say instead: "I'm just so angry with you that you never say no to your mother. She's ending up in charge of our life. I feel like I can't be close to you anymore because of your mother, and that scares me. When she calls tonight to arrange to go with us to look for our dining room furniture, will you tell her that we want to do this alone? I really just want to be with you when we make decisions about our house." Here Wendy says that she is angry without attacking anyone or demanding anything. Even if Mike is not ready to give her what she wants, he is more likely to hear what she's saying and so be able to think about it. By making Mike the center of her thoughts and words, she tells him that he—not his mother—is most important to her. This is a positive message we all like to hear.

TRAP #2: HAVING ALL-NIGHT "DISCUSSIONS"

Another alluring trap is the marathon encounter session, also known as "We stayed up all night having a discussion," or "We talked about that for several hours." All-nighters are seductive, even if the topic is unpleasant, because a marathon makes you feel alert as adrenaline surges and you experience moments of intense pain and pleasure. At least for that moment you feel that he needs you and that he is yours, that there is some hope that you may get what you want from him. The next day, however, you feel exhausted and unsure if anything has changed.

Tammy felt all of this when she and Don would discuss their problems for hours—sometimes over the phone because he traveled a lot, sometimes in person. As long as she kept talking she felt there was some hope for change; when they stopped, she felt despair. Marathon sessions are addictive because they set off a vicious cycle. They keep away feelings we don't want to have, so we never want to stop them. The primary feelings marathons block are separation feelings—the stark realization that you are separate and perhaps different from your man and that he is more different than you had expected. This feeling is especially difficult to tolerate because it stirs up all your feelings about past separations and moments when you were abandoned and disappointed. The despair that Tammy feels when she stops an all-night session comes from two different but powerful experiences: her early abandonment when her mother was hospitalized for two months and she was left with uncaring relatives, and Don's stubbornness. It is also important to keep in mind that even though he tells her that it's all her fault, he needs these endless discussions as much as Tammy does. (Women often act as the emotional educator and teacher during these talks, which is why you may feel depleted.) Feeling despair does not necessarily mean that your relationship ought to end or that you are a fool for staying in it. What it does indicate is that you and he got together to feel as one person and that you are both fearful of taking the next step—being together as two separate individuals. When you cut down your marathon discussion time, you may experience some anxiety, so be sure that you both reassure each other of your love. Don't forget that those marathons you may now long for weren't effective communications but blocks to the kind of real communication you're working toward now. With less time and energy wasted in marathons, you can now spend your time together doing things you enjoy, such as taking walks or listening to music. Make it a point not to reduce the number of times you bring up your feelings about the problems in your relationships. Dropping out of the marathon doesn't mean that you stop discussing your feelings, only that you do so in a different way. By keeping these conversations brief, you have a better chance of being heard.

TRAP #3: THE NEED TO BE RIGHT

"I'd rather be right than be president," said Henry Clay. And most of us agree that we'd rather be right more than anything else—especially during an argument. This presents another trap. You may think that men need to be right even more than you do, but when discussing their problems, both sexes work hard to score points with an invisible referee. Being right is extremely important to all of us because we all need approval, and in our world, being right often earns us approval—from parents, teachers, colleagues, and just about anyone else whose opinion of us matters. Countless couples in therapy have turned to me in the midst of an argument for a sign saying who is right, who is wrong, and by inference, who is good and who is bad. You may have even turned to a stranger to settle an argument about which couch to buy or where that restaurant is located—and then felt pleased if you were right, upset if you were wrong. There is an underlying assumption that we will be liked, even loved, if we are right, and disliked, even shunned, if we are wrong. If you need to be "right" in an argument, it may be because you were treated harshly by your parents when you were "wrong" and received physical or emotional punishment. If it was your fault that the kitchen got messed up, you felt as if you were unlovable. This kind of inappropriately harsh reaction from one's parents can leave the lasting impression that mistakes are unforgivable, and that you will only be loved if you are "right." All of us yearn for the unqualified approval of our parents, and if we don't get it, we desperately seek it throughout life from parent figures. We know that as romantic partners, you and the man in your life fill in, at times, as the other's substitute parents. So, in an argument where feelings should come first, you are each instead trying to prove that you are right (and thus lovable). Karen and Ron argued in this fruitless fashion.

Karen and Ron were married for six years before they had their first child, a boy named Manny. Though money was scarce—he taught at a community college, she at a nursery school—neither wanted to wait any longer to start a family. When Karen stopped working after Manny's birth, they just managed to get by and there was no extra money for baby-sitters or housekeepers. After six months she resumed part-time work but still was primarily responsible for their son. Their arguments concerned who would get up on weekend mornings to take care of Manny. Karen says, "I'm getting up early every morning to get Manny ready for the baby-sitter. It's not fair that I'm the one to get up on Saturdays too. You don't do half the work around here that I do. I'm exhausted and can't stand it anymore."

Ron responds, "What do you mean, I don't do half the work? I bring home twice as much money as you do, and I take care of him twice a week in the afternoons while you're at school. I'm certainly as hard-working as you are."

Karen and Ron have reached a stalemate. Both need to prove that they are good parents, hardworking and responsible. Each feels right and entitled to praise and a pat on the back as well as some time off. What they are vying for so desperately is approval and understanding, and this single-minded concern makes each deaf to the other. Neither dares to give the other any approval or to acknowledge that the other one might, in fact, be "right." To them that would be the same as giving in on the Saturday-morning battle. Needless to say, as long as Karen and Ron maintain their positions, nothing will change and things may actually get worse.

Most people are quite surprised to learn that it is, however, possible to acknowledge the other person's point of view and still maintain your position on what you want. Appreciation and understanding is what they both crave. It would be easier for Karen and Ron to resolve the weekend morning childcare problem if they could stop trying to be "right" and try, instead, to see how much they have in common, feeling-wise. One other reason why you insist on being right during an argument is that you may feel that you are entitled to be angry only if you are right. In this obsession to be right, Karen and Ron are missing out on a prime opportunity to be close through the feelings they have in common. Right now they feel exhausted and want someone else to take care of *them* for a change. Neither was prepared for the work involved in raising a child and making a living. They are overwhelmed. Feelings have nothing to do with being right or being wrong. They develop in our unconscious mind and are neither governed by rules of logic nor affected by whether our position is right or wrong. Karen need not feel she is "right" in order to be entitled to feel angry that Ron is not taking over for her on weekend mornings. When you and he insist on establishing right and wrong during your discussions, you are also blocking the free flow of feelings between you. Karen does not have to convince Ron that her point of view is accurate. She can even empathize with how tired he feels and appreciate how hard he works and still insist that she needs this time off.

Acknowledge your anger, whether you think it's right or wrong. We know that repressed anger causes massive interference in communication. In these exchanges you must also accept his angry feelings, and that means that you will want to bring your own protective shield. It can help to repeat these phrases to yourself:

"I am not wrong or bad because he is angry at me."

"If he gets this off his chest, we may be able to work out a solution afterward."

"His anger comes from the past too."

"He's angry about more than just this problem. It's not all my fault."

TRAP #4: POWER STRUGGLES

Wanting to win is as American as baseball and Mother's Day, and many of us believe that winning truly is everything.

The game doesn't count unless you take home the trophy. You have probably fallen into this trap—during arguments and discussions with your mate.

Edward and Fay are well skilled in power struggles. One of their favorite topics is Edward's wardrobe. Fay has felt embarrassed about the cheap, poorly made clothes that he has insisted on wearing since they met seven years ago, and she knows that money is not the problem. When she bought him nicer things, he reverted back to wearing his old favorites. She has also tried fighting with him about this, especially when they're going out together. She says, "Why do you insist on wearing that shirt when you know how much I hate it? The shirt doesn't even fit you right. Can't you wear the blue sweater I gave you last Christmas?"

Edward replies, "There you go again, telling me what to do. You're the most controlling woman I ever met. You want to tell me how to brush my teeth too? I like these clothes a lot better than those dainty ones you bought."

Fay sincerely wants Edward to look more attractive, and he is aware that the clothes that Fay suggests are a better choice. Fay also knows that the harder she tries to get Edward to change, the more he resists. He knows he's being stubborn, but he can't stop. Sometimes he would almost like to follow Fay's suggestions, but he can't bear the thought of her gloating over her success. These dynamics are typical of all power struggles, whether you are quarreling over housework, sex, or where to go on Friday night. The two parties become obsessed with each other and each strives to control the situation. Ironically, the more they struggle for control, the less control they have.

Power struggles begin early in life for all of us. The "terrible twos" that frazzled parents complain of is one of the first of these power struggles, as the child seeks to define who he is and what he wants by using a new word—"no." How our parents handle these contests and their own feelings about them affects the way that we deal with authorities as an adult. Edward's and Fay's past experiences determine how they behave today. For instance, when Edward was young, his father openly disdained any man who took pains with his wardrobe, calling them "sissies" and making it clear that Edward's mother would not boss *him* around about clothes or anything else. When Edward's mother dressed him nicely, his father mocked him, and when Edward tried to change for his father, his mother became upset. Although Edward could see then, as well as now, that his mother and Fay know more about clothing than his father, he can't help but feel that he loses his father's love and his identity as a man when he "gives in" to Fay. We use power struggles in an attempt to maintain our identity when it seems that outside forces are trying to take over. Since Edward's parents were insecure about who they were and felt weak, they couldn't learn from each other without fear of losing their sense of self. Edward has the same problem.

Fay, on the other hand, seeks to control because she is anxious. Her family was usually in chaos because neither parent could keep order and her brother was in trouble during his teens. Fay was praised only when she stepped in to solve problems, but was otherwise ignored while her parents were preoccupied with her brother. In this unstructured and neglectful environment, Fay sought to take care of things out of her frustration and because her parents requested this in different ways. Edward represents Fay's "problem brother," whom she must help no matter how hopeless the task may be, while Fay is Edward's mother, who challenges his masculinity. Fay can influence Edward, but first she must use a different approach—noninterference. When she stops trying so hard to control (as Edward views her), Edward will feel freer to make his own choices rather than resorting to this "If you say black, I'll say white" routine. If Fay realizes that healthy egos usually make the best choices when they have support, not when they're under pressure, she can relax and just suggest things to Edward and compliment him when she thinks he looks attractive.

Finding yourself in a power struggle with your mate should prompt you to examine your family history to see if you, like Fay, are still carrying out your parents' wishes to assume responsibility for a "difficult child." Could you be trying to fix your father's defects? Or work harder and harder in a bid to get the love you missed as a child? Even if you succeed in forcing your man to change before he wants to, the anger he carries away with him could return in another form. Billie Holiday, the famous blues singer, addressed this situation when she said, "Sometimes it's worse to win a fight than to lose."

TRAP #5: HOLDING GRUDGES

Grudge holding, keeping private mental lists of all the ways in which your man has done you wrong, can feel satisfying and safe. You remember what he's done, even if he doesn't. The writer Dorothy Parker told us that "women and elephants never forget." Similarly, grudge holders never forget disappointments, insults, lateness, or criticisms, though they might forget the compliments, warm moments, and special favors they received. If you are a grudge holder, you keep this secret list of wrongdoings for several reasons. First and foremost, you protect the man in your life from knowing your true feelings and you protect yourself from his reaction. You think that the relationship will end if he hears the full extent of what you feel or that his anger toward you will be intolerable, so you don't tell him. But you still remember. Second, you keep this list so that if he ever leaves you or complains about you, you have ammunition. Third, you have decided that expressing yourself is a waste of your emotions because it will get you nowhere; besides, "He's not going to change anyway." Even though you may say that, you can't stop yourself from noticing, feeling, and memorizing every hurt and disappointment. You may hold a grudge because you haven't said what it is that you feel, but some women hold grudges even after they've said everything. They carry their hurt and anger long after the argument ends. Even during good times, their anger and indignation prevent them from enjoying their men. You hold grudges more because it is a habit than because you really want to.

Alison has been holding grudges since she started dating men without really knowing why. With her high school boyfriend she would sulk until he started a fight that led to a confession of the problem. The two relationships she had in college each lasted two years, and when she broke them off, she never told the men about her list. Now, at age twenty-eight Alison has become concerned about why her relationships don't last as long as the fund-raising jobs she's had. However, she remembers every time Max, her boyfriend of one year, has been late or forgotten appointments. Secretly she is furious at him and doesn't know if she could stand being married to him, which is what he says he wants.

If you met Alison, she would remind you of sweetness and goodness. Even when she feels upset and talks about it, her anger barely shows. She is like her mother, whom everyone described as the "sweetest woman in the world" and who worked around Alison's father's explosive, sometimes violent temper, which he expressed toward the children. Alison's mother died a few years ago of a stroke after a lifetime of diabetes. Alison keeps her grudge list because expressions of feelings were not welcomed in her family. Her resentments, hurts, disappointments, and anger are kept in her head. Her "memory bank" was vital to her well-being in her family, but now it is outmoded and serves no purpose. Alison will feel more like marrying Max if she realizes that she is not "the sweetest woman in the world" and that her private feelings gradually need to be made public if she wants to make room for love to grow.

If you are the other kind of grudge holder, who says what she feels but then holds on to the anger anyway for days or weeks, it may help if you realize that this is a habit that can be broken. Calming exercises such as meditation, relaxation, or physical exercise can help to distract you. Doing anything that makes you feel good about yourself can also help to disperse the anger. You can also break the angry mood by telling your man in a humorous or pleasant way that you're still angry but that you're trying hard to get rid of it so that you can be with

him. Keeping intellectual lists of the problems that have occurred between you and the man in your life *is* important. You
can't learn from history unless you remember it. But when you
hold on to the feelings that go with this history—which is a
way to punish your man and hold back on love—you will be
the loser.

TRAP #6: GUILT

As if it were not hard enough to forge a relationship with
a difficult man, along comes guilt, the feeling that you are to
blame for something. Feeling guilt is an exhausting, draining
experience. You can actually feel "ripped apart by guilt," torn
between what you know is good and right for *you* and what
it is that your mate wants. Dr. Willard Gaylin, a noted psychoanalyst, in his book *Feelings,* explains further why guilt can be
so destructive. "True guilt seeks, indeed embraces, punishment." It is ". . . between us and ourselves." Guilt, then, can
be a way of punishing yourself when, instead of fulfilling the
"traditional" woman's role as a soother and supporter, you
have been angry or upset or firm about what you need from
your man. If you were raised to feel protective of your parents
and responsible for their happiness or physical well-being, you
will be even more susceptible to feeling guilty when you take
care of yourself.

Trudy, for example, in the many years she's been married to Harold, has played the role of good listener and
helpmate. This year, however, as a result of returning to
school for her advanced degree, and a part-time editing
job, she's feeling more confident and less willing to listen

to Harold's daily narrations. She has told him that she feels her daily activities are as interesting as his, and he has obliged by asking her questions and acting interested in her day. But Trudy feels so guilty and uncomfortable when he gives her the attention she specifically asked for that she rushes through their conversations. Further contributing to her guilt feelings, Trudy's mother, who expected her to take care of her when she got older, has wanted to live with them since Trudy's father died last year. This has not happened because Harold forbids it. But still Trudy feels guilty.

Guilt is a spoiler. It deprives Trudy of enjoying her newly discovered separateness and individual achievements. Guilt is also a substitute emotion for other feelings. Behind the massive guilt, Trudy wrestles with fear, hurt, disappointment, and rage. She is afraid that she will be unloved if she does not give all or most of her attention to others. She is hurt and disappointed that her mother and Harold aren't more interested in her, and she even questions how real their love for her is. Lastly, she is furious that after giving them so much, she has to ask to be treated similarly in return. What makes these feelings so risky is that they are directed toward other people. Guilt feels safe because it is directed only at yourself. For Trudy to get what she wants—and keep it—she must replace her guilt with these other feelings. It's a risk worth taking. Unchecked guilt will prevent you from getting what you want and leave you resentful.

Therapists also talk of "induced" feelings—those feelings produced in people by their relationships with other people. Although Harold has agreed to listen to Trudy talk about herself, he often resents doing it and does not mind when Trudy rushes to change the focus of the conversation from herself. Trudy observes this, but instead of bringing up her anger and hurt, she expresses the induced feeling of guilt. Both Trudy and Harold feel a strong pull to maintain the status quo rather than risk change and growth. Guilt is part of the tug backward that Trudy feels. Robert Louis Stevenson said, "What hangs people . . . is the unfortunate circumstances of guilt." Though we hope that criminals will "hang themselves" through their guilt, don't let guilt over claiming what is rightfully yours hang you.

TRAP #7: FALLING FOR HIS DIVERSIONS

Creating diversions is an old trick used by armies to draw attention and manpower away from the primary target. Your man may use a whole array of diversions (unconsciously) to distract you from your goal and make you expend energy so it's not there when you need it. Knowing what these diversions are helps you recognize them and maintain your fixed course. The two most frequently encountered diversions are *emotional overreactions* and *dead-end responses*.

Emotional overreactions can be manifested in many ways, from sulking to screaming. But no matter how he does it, your man ends up stealing the show away from your feelings. The original issue that you raised gets lost in the commotion. For example, here's what happened to Wendy and Matt.

After living with Matt for four years, Wendy knows that he admires her intelligence and listens to her opinion on a variety of issues. So she has been especially upset and hurt when Matt is harshly critical of her opinions in front of other people. Because she doesn't want to fight in front of others, she waits until they are alone before mentioning how she feels. But each time she tells Matt that she is hurt and furious and embarrassed that he is putting her down in public, he calls her a "complaining woman." He says, "It's about time somebody told you how wrong you are. You shouldn't go shooting your mouth off about everything when you don't know what you're talking about." He is enraged as he goes on and usually winds up walking away from her, wherever they are. This scene is then followed by an angry silence from Matt that can last all day. Out of frustration and loneliness Wendy goes to Matt and talks him out of his sulk. The original problem—his public criticism of her—is forgotten until the next time.

Matt's tantrums obscure the real issue. Although Wendy doesn't know why he is doing it, she needs to stop this diversion as quickly as possible. She should *not* try to find out why he feels the way he does, because his response is irrational and inappropriate to the situation, and her probing will only move them further away from resolving the issue of his public criticisms. What Wendy can tell Matt is this: "You're only making me angrier when you attack me like this and then get silent. I'm the one who has been put down in public, not you. You've got to stop criticizing me in public because it is affecting how I feel about you. How about waiting till we're alone and let me know then?" Matt, in fact, is doing what he used to do as a child when he had been "bad." He is placing the blame onto someone else. He did this because punishment in his home usually meant "getting a beating" or getting the silent treatment—neither of which he could stand. If Matt continues to criticize Wendy in front of others, she can try telling him right on the spot that she does not like this (after all, he's the one who ought to feel embarrassed, not her), or she can leave the particular gathering. In any case, she, and you, should not let this kind of diversion, an emotional overreaction, stop you from expressing your feelings and changing the situation. He will respect you more if you refuse to cater to his tantrums.

Dead-end responses are dramatic. You have just told your man how upset you are, and he says: "I guess I'm just no good," or "I can't do anything right," or "That's just the way I am. Take it or leave it," or "At my age, you can't expect me to change," or "My father was like this too. I guess it's just in the blood." These are called dead-end responses because they make you feel closed out and hopeless. They are designed (unconsciously) to distract your attention by shocking you and so end the discussion. Perhaps you try to reassure him that he's better than he thinks, or you try convincing him that he's not too old to change, or that just because his father was like this doesn't mean that he can't be different. These are all sympathetic, supportive statements that your man will surely like to hear. The problem with them is, however, that they put you in the position of helping *him,* rather than getting *him* to help *you.* Men who give dead-end responses are very much absorbed with their own problems and have difficulty being aware of their mate's feelings. They usually come from families where the mother never clearly stated what she needed. It is important for you to ring a bell to wake up your mate to your emotional existence and your specific needs, since he did not learn to do this at home. One way to ring a bell is to give his exact words back to him, like a tape recorder replaying his statement ("You guess you're just no good?"). Another method is to ask him "How is what you said going to help this problem we have?" Another similar reflective question is "What am I supposed to do when you make a statement like that? Stop talking, get angry with you, give up, find someone else to be with?" These kinds of replies will reshape your relationship and get him to think about you instead of himself. In the long run, the work that you do to become psychologically aware of yourself and your man and the communication traps that lie before you, will enhance your self-confidence when he is at his worst.

~~~~~~~~~~

The Man Who Puts Up Walls: Uncovering His Emotional Side

~~~~~~~~~~

The basic discovery about any people is the discovery of the relationship between its men and women.

—PEARL S. BUCK

There is only one sex. . . . A man and a woman are so entirely the same thing that one can scarcely understand the subtle reasons for sex distinction with which our minds are filled.

—GEORGE SAND

MEN are strong and silent, brave and courageous, or unfeeling brutes; a man you can count on, a man you can trust —the usual descriptions of a "real" man make him sound suspiciously like a marble statue. You know that he'll always be there, but you'll never know what he feels, or if he feels anything at all. Many women think that they are living with a statue when they ask the man in their life "What do you feel?" He freezes, becomes mute, stares at the floor vacantly. A silence that threatens to last into eternity surrounds you. Perhaps he makes a joke, changes the subject, or walks away. It's not surprising that women have given up in despair, concluding that maybe he really doesn't have feelings "like a woman" or, if he does, "he'll never tell me." As a result of repeated experiences like these, as well as other causes, many of us have come to accept as fact the myth that men are unemotional. Since we can't see or hear his feelings, we assume they do not exist. If tears are not shed, there is no pain. If his hands don't tremble, there is no fear. Thinking that your uncommunicative man must not have feelings as you do, you hesitate to feel close to or trust him when you need him. The emotional woman living with her unemotional man feels isolated.

Vicki and Vinnie have shared the same house for the twenty years they've been married. They have a son and daughter, and they are both musicians; he plays violin with an orchestra and she teaches the piano. According to Vicki, however, they've never shared the same feeling about anything serious because, she says, Vinnie doesn't feel. She offers many examples of this. When Vicki has had an argument with their son about his school behavior, she feels very upset. Vinnie typically says, "What are you getting so upset about? I had problems in school, too, and I turned out okay." Vicki doesn't agree with this assessment, but she stays quiet on the subject. Sometimes she cries because of a hurtful remark Vinnie has made. At those moments he invariably laughs. Whereas she finds her work draining and frustrating, he loves what he does and can't understand why she doesn't just find the right job and enjoy it. Vicki says everyone likes Vinnie —always outgoing, rarely blue. He doesn't even get angry at the things that upset most people, while she has entire angry days. On rare occasions Vinnie will blow his stack (usually at the kids) and then he might put his fist through the wall or kick a chair around. Vicki feels scared when this happens and even more alienated from him. She's never exploded like that in her life and thinks he's nuts to do it. Vicki's resigned to being the emotional one in the family—feeling "every little thing." She's never tried to get Vinnie to be more sensitive to her or expressive. Instead, she complains about him to women friends; sometimes they make her feel better. But she feels lonely and sad with Vinnie a lot of the time. The distance between them never gets closer.

Every time his feelings arise, Vinnie says something to push Vicki away from him and away from her emotions. No wonder she has concluded that her husband does not have similar feelings, that they are just too different. But Vinnie's excessively negative reaction to expressed feelings actually gives away his secret: He feels everything and it overwhelms him. His fragile sense of well-being would be toppled easily if he should acknowledge to himself or to Vicki that indeed, he is as upset as she is about their son, about frustrations at work, about his explosive temper. As he sees it, admitting these thoughts to anyone would make him a "pushover," a "weak guy." Over fifty years ago Dr. Mabel Ulrich wrote that although a man may elevate his knowledge and put down his feelings ". . . only about ten percent of him is his intellect— the other ninety his emotions." But even if he is ninety percent emotional, how are you to know what he feels, or that he

213

feels at all if he never tells you? Vicki thinks she would have to be Superwoman to penetrate Vinnie's tough-guy or easygoing facade. But even without x-ray vision you can decipher what your apparently unemotional man feels and, over time, help him to express this or at least to be responsive to you. Before we look for the key to unlock his emotional secrets, let's review why he hides his feelings from you and the rest of the world.

Why He Hides, and What You Can Do

1. He is afraid that he will be rejected by you, criticized for being an inadequate man who does not have the "strong back" on which you need to lean. If the man in your life is like Vinnie, he will need to hear many times from you that you will not leave him if he reveals his sensitivity and that you admire him for being strong enough to be aware of his feelings.

2. He has never had as a role model a man who is emotionally close to others yet maintains a sense of himself. Vinnie's father, for instance, was even more silent than Vinnie on emotional subjects and would leave the room when his mother got upset.

3. He fears he will lose control of his feelings, and thus his life, once he lets down the wall that protects his sensitive core. He may also think that you will be as overwhelmed by his emotions as he is. Reassure him that what he feels can't be any more upsetting to you than what you go through when he doesn't seem to feel at all.

214

4. He seeks to balance your emotional ways with his emotionless approach, so that "things don't get out of hand." He may even accuse you of being out of control when you express what you feel. This probably comes from his family experience, and he assumes that you are the same (as his mother, in Vinnie's case). Tell him that you don't require a stabilizing influence—that although you express yourself, you're not going "off your rocker" and neither will he if he just says what he feels and tells you what he needs.

5. He is in the habit of cutting off communication when his feelings are aroused. You ignite the emotional part of him when you express yourself, and he automatically rushes in to squelch the feeling with a laugh or a cutting remark. Your response to his old habits can be "I'd prefer if you didn't laugh when I'm upset. I know you feel upset, too, by what I'm saying, but it would be better if you just tell me that you'd like me to stop crying because you can't handle it."

6. He is afraid of the intimate feelings he will have if he drops his "tough-guy" pose. Although he is already dependent on you (and you on him), he may feel that once he lets you in on his secret—that he's a feeling person —he "will need you too much." You might tell him that you hope both of you can be close but remain able to survive alone. It won't help your relationship to be enslaved to each other.

These, then, are the six basic reasons why your man hides his emotional self: fear of rejection, lack of role models, fear of losing control, trying to maintain a balance, as a result of old habits, and a fear of intimacy and dependency. None of these problems should be a stranger to you, and your task of reaching him will be easier if you admit that you have the same fears and difficulties.

The man who puts up walls is highly skilled at keeping his inner emotional life hidden from the world. Just as the un-trained eye will not see the wildlife hidden in the thick jungle, you will not see the signs of your man's camouflaged feelings until you have learned to discern them. Although it looks as if he has never experienced anxiety, jealousy, or insecurity, you can become expert at tracking the clues he leaves for you every day. These will indicate that, in fact, he feels all these things, just as you do. Here, then, is another job for you to undertake in your struggle to love this difficult man. This extra work that you are taking on, however, will have a direct influence on your level of self-confidence. For example, if you think that you are alone in feeling anxious, you may be critical of yourself. But if you know that he can be as anxious as you are, you will feel more confident and comfortable with your own feelings. Let us examine what signs and clues to look for, and how to master reading the meaning of it all.

Reading Emotional Sign Language

An archaeologist may spend a lifetime interpreting the pic-tures on cave walls—hieroglyphics—in order to understand an ancient civilization. He looks for the hidden meaning behind the written symbols. You want to find the hidden meaning behind your man's behavior and empty words, the hieroglyph-ics or emotional sign language he communicates to you every day. Frequently you will have to ignore the actual words he has spoken in order to understand the meaning, especially when what he has said makes no sense to you or seems inappropriate.

Let's look at an example. You and your mate are out jogging together. Preoccupied with problems at work, you fail to hear the bell of a bicycle coming up behind you and narrowly miss being hit by a racing cyclist. Your man moved you out of harm's way just in the nick of time. Once he realizes that you are fine, he says, "What the hell is wrong with you? Didn't you hear him?" You immediately feel hurt and angry. Wasn't it bad enough that you had almost been hit? Couldn't he be sympathetic or blame it on the crazy cyclist? You think to yourself once again how cruel and unfeeling he is. You yell back at him and feel unloved for the rest of the morning.

How much better you would feel if you understood that behind his cruel words is love for you. First ask yourself: Why did he speak to me in such an inappropriately angry manner? A clue lies in the intensity of his anger. You will realize that he actually felt terrified that you were so close to danger—and guilty that he had not protected you better. His very intense anger hides his equally intense fear and need for you to be safe. Once you know this, you will feel less hurt, angry, and estranged from him. You will be better equipped to talk to him about the incident. As always, remember that understanding him emotionally does not mean that you ignore your own hurt. Once you know that beneath his anger he cares, you can reach out to him in a more understanding way when you ask for what you want: not to be attacked by his anxiety and fear.

Here are several more examples in which the man puts up walls that make him appear on the surface to be emotionless, insensitive, or hurtful. We will uncover the hidden messages his behavior conveys and then determine what you can do in each situation. The men described here never talk about their feelings and they are not consciously aware of these hidden messages we will find.

THE DINNER SITUATION

Mary usually does the cooking at home, but every once in a while Frank agrees to shop for or cook dinner. Mary notices that every time he does this he either buys the wrong ingredients or burns the dinner. Mary thinks he's just a birdbrain in the kitchen and envies her friends whose husbands know their way around a stove. She sees Frank's behavior here as just one more example of how she lost out by marrying him.

THE HIDDEN MESSAGE

Frank agrees to shop and cook, but, in fact, he is angry about doing those chores. His spoiling the dinner each and every time he undertakes the task is the clue here. Underneath his amiable and "simple" (as Mary sees him) surface, he is resentful and feels pushed around and used by her. He may also feel insecure about his culinary abilities compared to Mary's.

THE FAMILY VISIT SITUATION

Walter says that he enjoys going to visit Susan's folks, yet the last time they attended a family gathering, Walter was late picking up Susan (they're engaged but live apart) and "dressed like a slob." Because this was a special family occasion, Susan was upset and thought to herself, "He is a social idiot. How will I ever be able to marry him? I'll have to pick out all his clothes."

Despite what he says, Walter really does not want to go to the family affair. He is upset with Susan's mother because she does not like him, and he feels insecure and angry because the family does not talk to him much when he's there. Dressing down is his unconscious way of "putting down" her family.

THE AIRPORT SITUATION

Alice has been away on a two-week business trip. Her husband, Morris, says he doesn't mind these occasional trips, claiming that it gives him a chance to catch up on his reading and his woodworking projects. Still, every time Alice flies home and he agrees to meet her, something goes wrong and he's never there when she gets in. She waits for forty-five minutes and then goes home mad. He arrives home two hours later, even madder, because he's been waiting for three hours in the wrong spot. Alice thinks that Morris is just too selfish and irresponsible. Why couldn't he even bother to look around for her instead of standing in one spot waiting for her to find him? He never makes her feel secure, or that she can count on him. Alice thinks she won't ask him to pick her up at the airport anymore.

THE HIDDEN MESSAGE
What Morris says and what he feels are totally opposite. When Alice goes on one of these trips, Morris feels very abandoned. Since she's becoming so successful at work, he has worried that she will meet someone else. The clue here is his strange behavior at the airport—his not looking for her. Unconsciously he wanted Alice to look for *him* so that he would feel needed for a change. Morris feels much like the wife

who's been left at home, where she's bored and taken for granted.

THE FRIEND SITUATION

Naomi is very upset because her dear friend at work is moving to another state, and at dinner she tells her husband, George, about it. Without commenting on Naomi's problem, George breaks right in with a story about a friend he met on the street that day who he hadn't seen in a while. Naomi is hurt and furious. George seems to want to talk only about himself and ignores her feelings. She tells him he's "self-centered and unfeeling."

THE HIDDEN MESSAGE

George is scared by Naomi's feelings of abandonment. The callous way that he interrupts her signals that he is feeling something he's not saying. He has never admitted to himself that he feels abandoned by anyone, but deep down he feels hurt about past losses. He is overwhelmed by the openness of Naomi's words and so, unconsciously, quickly changes the subject to avoid his own feelings. He may also be jealous that Naomi has a friend who means so much to her. Mentioning his own friend is his way of saying, "You see, I have friends too."

In each situation, the man says or does the "wrong" thing, causing the woman to feel hurt, angry, and alienated. The woman cannot understand "why he would do or say such a stupid thing," and the distance and mistrust between them grows. If you are willing to take on the complicated job of searching for the hidden message, you can help your mate

2 2 0

become aware that he has an inner feeling life that he ignores. And when he ignores these feelings, he becomes hurtful and difficult to live with. In fact, when you tell him this you are complimenting him, suggesting that there is more to him than he realizes. More important, he can become more emotionally responsive to you. Hopefully, you can bring a halt to the hurtful things he says and does. You and your relationship can grow because as you recognize more of his true feelings you will see more of your own. You may eventually be in agreement with Ivy Compton-Burnett, who said, "There is more difference within the sexes than between them." An extra added benefit to keep in mind is that quite often men (and women) become more successful in their careers when the women in their life reaches out to this hidden inner feeling self. Once you know what the hidden messages are, there are several routes you can take to communicate what you know and what you want.

Reaching the Man Behind the Wall

In each of the above situations, the woman has several options open to her once she understands the hidden message. She can

1. ask questions and/or

2. make statements, or

3. keep silent.

For example, in the Dinner Situation, Mary knows that Frank is angry and resentful about making dinner, and possibly insecure about being a chef. She can ask, in a kindly way, a question that relates his feelings to his actions: "Do you think that you're angry about making dinner, and that's why there's a problem every time?" A statement might include her feelings too: "I'm feeling anxious when you agree to make dinner because there's a problem every time. I love that you're cooking and want you to keep at it. But I think you must be resenting it and that's why something goes wrong. Maybe if you talk about what you feel, things will get better and I can relax and enjoy the dinner." The third alternative, silence, is not as useless as it sounds. Mary knows from reading his sign language that Frank is angry but trying to please her anyway, and understanding this can be somewhat comforting. If she tolerates the burnt dinners and forgotten ingredients silently, it is likely that Frank eventually will express anger or frustration himself. Mary should not try to be helpful when this happens, but listen to his feelings. Once Frank gets his feelings off his chest, the dinners should improve.

In the Family Visit Situation Susan knows from reading Walter's emotional signs that he feels insecure and angry about visiting her family, especially her mother. She can express herself in one of these ways:

Question: "Do you think that you were late and dressed badly because you're annoyed about visiting my family? I'd love you to come with me, but would you prefer not to go, since it upsets you?"

Statement: "I feel angry at you when you express your feelings by being late and dressing like you don't care. I'd rather hear your feelings directly if you're angry or upset. If you don't want to go see my family, then just say so ahead of time. I'll be disappointed, but it's better than fighting at the last minute about how late you are, or about your clothes."

Silence: Saying nothing when your mate is late and dressed as if he's going to wash his car is not easy. If you can manage to keep quiet about either behavior, he will probably realize what he's done anyway. However, before the next family event, discuss how he feels about going, and whether or not he really wants to attend. Perhaps you can arrange to meet him there instead of being kept waiting again.

Whichever form of communication you use, express clearly that there is a relationship between his provocative behavior and his underlying hidden feelings, and that his behavior evokes feelings in you too. The Airport Situation provides an especially good opportunity to become more intimate if Alice is willing to decipher Morris's hidden message. Here's what she can say.

Question: "Do you think that you didn't search for me at the airport because you're upset that I went away again and left you? Could it be that you wanted me to chase after you and make you feel wanted?"

Statement: "I'm annoyed that you didn't look for me at the airport, but think you're angry and worried about these trips I'm taking and that's why you didn't bother. I'd much rather we talked about our feelings than play games at the airport. I'm feeling insecure that you'll meet someone while I'm away, and I think you're feeling that same way about me. I think we need to reassure each other about our relationship."

Silence: Knowing that Morris is obviously upset about her business trips, Alice can choose to keep this information to herself. She can reflect on her own feelings about being separated from Morris. Before her next trip she should tell Morris that she wants to maintain closer contact while she is away because she misses him. More frequent phone calls or letters could be the answer. Morris will not feel so abandoned and will feel more secure so that he can show Alice how much he missed her once she has said that she needs him too.

Most "mistakes" that he makes or comments that seem rude or self-centered or just downright nasty can be interpreted to mean several different things. One possible meaning, of course, is that each situation indicates the hostility that he feels but keeps locked up inside. However, every situation can also be seen as an invitation to open up a dark room to the warm light, to take a problem and understand the deeper feelings that are inside it, to become more intimate. Even if you two get into an argument because you have probed beneath the surface, the open expression of unpleasant feelings between you, and then the speedy return to warmth, should reinforce the bond between you. Alice's airport problem with Morris helped them to become closer once she understood his hidden feelings of insecurity and abandonment and his silent request for closer contact while she was away. To achieve this, Alice had to admit first that she needed Morris and be secure enough to ask Morris to admit the same. Finding deep in yourself the feelings that are similar to his and using this knowledge to open him up is what I call parallel talking.

Parallel Talking

Parallel talking can pry open the locks on your man's emotional life. This situation with a man who is the Great Denier, will show how parallel talking works.

Izzy loves to talk. That's one of his attributes that attracted Christine to him eight years ago. He loves to tell jokes or anecdotes, and he enjoys being the expert —talking about one of the areas where he is knowledgeable—on insurance (his business), trout fishing, or antique cars. What Izzy is *not* an expert about are his feelings. The other night Izzy was unusually quiet, and Christine asked him if anything was wrong. He said no. As the night wore on, Christine became more uneasy with Izzy's silence. When she insisted that something *must* be wrong, Izzy got annoyed and finally said, "What's wrong is your bothering me." Christine asked more specific questions. She asked, "How did work go today?" Izzy replied, "Fine. Oh, they told Fred he was going to take that trip out west, so I guess he's getting the new account." Now Christine understood why Izzy had been so quiet. She asked him how he felt about this. He answered, as usual, that it didn't bother him. Christine now felt doubly frustrated. She knew that Izzy was upset deep down, but he either didn't want to talk about it or he wasn't in touch with how upset he really was. Meanwhile, she was being deprived of his company and felt alone. She wished he would scream or shout or cry rather than deny everything and mope. And she didn't know what to do with *her* feelings about his lost account.

This dilemma is all too familiar for most women. Their usually talkative mate is moody and silent and won't even drop a hint as to the problem. In his silence, you, of course, can imagine all sorts of dreadful causes, each worse than the real problem. Christine, like a good detective, uncovered the clue to Izzy's mood by asking specific questions. She did this in a chatty, easy manner so that Izzy would not feel pressured or as if he were being interrogated. Though she now knows why he's silent (at other times his snappiness provides the clue), Christine doesn't know how to get him to open up so that they can share this crisis. In this situation you want desperately not to be closed off from all communication. Through parallel talking you can use your feelings and help him get in touch with his. Christine knows that Izzy feels angry and betrayed that he didn't get the account, though he denies this. She will parallel his feelings with her own by using one of these communications.

1. "If this happened to me at work, I would feel furious that somebody else got what I deserved."

2. "Even if you don't feel anything about what happened, I feel angry that they're treating you that way."

3. (In a kidding tone) "I know you don't feel angry about this, but I do. And it's not even my job!"

Since she is probably also upset because Izzy is so reluctant to talk, Christine might want to add:

4. "I don't believe that you don't feel anything at all about what happened at work—you're just keeping it all to yourself. I feel upset that you won't let me in on what you feel. After all, I tell you about my feelings all the time!"

And for a sweeter, less confrontational approach that might encourage him to talk:

5. "It would help me to feel closer to you and more relaxed when I'm with you if you would talk to me more about what's happened to you during the day, especially when it's something like this. If you don't like the way that I respond, then tell me what I can say that would help you."

Most men want you to reassure them that they can "handle the problem" when a crisis like Izzy's occurs. If you think he can handle it, then he thinks he can too. Thus Christine could say:

6. "I know you'll be able to get through this problem. If you don't get this account, you'll get the next one."

Always trust your intuition. If you "feel that something is going on" with him, then it probably is, whether he wants to talk about it or not. The man who puts up walls does so because he learned that this is how men "are supposed to behave" when they feel vulnerable. Says the psychologist Dr. J. Munder Ross: "Men who are insecure . . . become hypermasculine to reassure themselves."

A final word of caution. If the man in your life reacts to parallel talking with anger, you may want to remain silent rather than reach out to him when he is moody. How involved you become depends on your willingness to tolerate his angry feelings toward you when you try to unblock his walled-off emotions. Though he becomes angry, in time he will be more emotionally open and responsive thanks to your efforts. You should never persist when he is verbally attacking or abusive, however. Remember, you are working to achieve feeling communication, not martyrdom.

Emotional Twinship

A difficult man often opposes you on every decision. You want to eat out—he's not hungry. You want to go to the movies—he doesn't. You want to make love—he's not interested in sex. You like to jog—he'd rather watch football on TV. You like ballet—he'd rather go to a boxing match. You are convinced that your differences are not only physical but mental as well. How, then, could he possibly be your emotional twin?

What I mean by the term "emotional twinship" is that you and your man possess very similar if not identical feelings deep within you, underneath the day-to-day surface reactions and behaviors that seem so contradictory. These unconscious identical feelings that you two share drew you together and hold you together more strongly than the obvious superficial attractions. These unconscious feelings are very elusive and hard to discern under the best of circumstances. In times of conflict it is impossible to uncover the feelings you have in common. Thus, the best time to observe the emotional twinship between you is when you are at peace.

The longer a woman lives with a man, the more she is able to understand the emotional twinship they share. Women tend to idealize men at the beginning of relationships, erroneously assuming that their man does not have the "weak" feelings that they have. As the years roll on, the woman becomes wiser, realizing, at least, that she was never really "weaker" than he.

The woman who comes to this awareness does so because she observes their daily life very carefully. You, too, can become a wise woman by using your powers of observation, just as these women have done.

Charles accuses Julia of being an overly jealous woman, and Julia admits that she feels jealous often. The last time they went to a party, she fumed for hours and said to Charles, "You spent an hour talking shop with a woman because she also sells antique furniture. But it looked to me like you were flirting, not working. You completely ignored me when I came over to join the conversation." Julia has decided that there is nothing wrong with her jealous feelings. She thinks that Charles, underneath his bluster about jealousy being infantile, is a very jealous man himself, but she never gives him an opportunity to feel it. At the next party Julia makes it a point to talk at length to an attractive man. She observes that Charles notices this and seems to be sulking in a corner for the rest of the party. When they get home, Charles sarcastically comments, "You seemed to be having a good time tonight." Julia asks him what he means though she already knows. When he asks, "Was that guy making a play for you?" Julia's suspicions are confirmed: Charles is as jealous as she is, no matter how he tries to hide it. She tells him that they are emotional twins when it comes to jealousy.

Patty and Mark are going to the Caribbean on vacation. Previously, any time there has been a snafu at the airport, it is Patty who gets upset, angry, and impatient with the airline staff. Mark tells her to "calm down and stop getting so excited—you're making a scene." He appears easygoing, carefree, and unconcerned. Patty doesn't think she's making a scene; she feels that she's justifiably upset and saying what needs to be said. She is sure that Mark is at least as impatient and angry as she is. She's seen the way he can be when there's a delay in service at a restaurant. This time, when they find out at the airport that they have no reservations, Patty makes sure to keep her thoughts to herself. She is not surprised to hear Mark yell at the staff in a far nastier tone than she would ever use. He even gets angry with her because she forced him to be "the bad guy." "I guess we both can get impatient and angry pretty quickly," Patty says to Mark. Though their outward responses seemed different, Patty and her man are emotional twins under the surface, just as she suspected.

Maurice doesn't like it when Margo acts, as he puts it, "clingy and needy." He accuses her of this when she keeps after him to "do things with her on the weekends," or when she is especially affectionate physically. Margo doesn't think that she is "clingy" nor does she see anything wrong with feeling needy. In fact, she wishes more people would admit that they felt that way, especially Maurice. Margo is sure that Maurice needs her just as much as she needs him, and in order to test her theory, she plans a few weekends seeing other friends, attending workshops, and visiting family. By the second weekend, Maurice is moping around the house and questioning her incessantly about her plans. They even have a fight. He is much more affectionate than usual when she returns from a workshop and finally admits that he misses her when she's away a lot. Margo tells Maurice that she's glad he can tell her he missed her—it makes her feel terrific. She thinks it took a lot of strength for Maurice to admit that. Margo is assured that Maurice is as "needy" of her as she is of him.

In these three cases, instead of criticizing themselves for being overly emotional and weak (as their men described them), each woman held fast to her feelings and tested out the emotional twinship theory. Each woman observed a pattern, changed her automatic response to a common situation to disrupt the pattern, and kept her feelings and observations to herself until she saw how her man reacted. When he then displayed the feelings of jealousy, anger, and need that she usually had in these situations instead, he revealed that under the surface they are indeed emotional twins. Men often take the opposite position, out of habit, on the assumption that a balance must be maintained. In their view, a relationship cannot have too much jealousy, too much anger, too much neediness. This psychological phenomenon is known as "complementarity." In a way, your man needs you to express these feelings for him. When you stop, he is forced to admit to these feelings himself, something he is usually scared to do. After you have observed your and your mate's emotional twinship many times, you will feel more confident in your emotions and freer to be yourself in the relationship even when he doesn't like your feelings. Continue explaining to him that from what you've seen, the two of you are more alike than different.

With all his blustering and bellowing, criticisms and silences that you endure as an emotional woman living with a difficult man who puts up walls, it may help to keep in mind what Henry David Thoreau said about his own sex: "I believe that men are generally still a little afraid of the dark, though the witches are all hung, and Christianity and candles have been introduced." When he complains because you are, at times, afraid, remember that underneath his bravado he also fears the dark.

—◆◆◆◆◆◆◆◆—

A Difficult Man Is Any Man: How To Love Him, and Why Bother

—◆◆◆◆◆◆◆◆—

Though his beginnings be but poor and low,
Thank God a man can grow!
                    —FLORENCE EARLE COATES

O Man, my former loves, how one gains and learns in your company!
                    —COLETTE

A difficult man can be any man – husband, father, lover, stranger or brother. And you can meet a difficult man anywhere – on the train, at dinner, in the office, or in the bedroom. You no doubt know several of these difficult men: Your boss who taught you so much yet doesn't want to promote you and let go. Your father who gazes at you warmly but never talks to you. Your brother who you pal around and laugh with but who gets himself into trouble, causes you worry, then ignores your advice. And a difficult man is your mate who at times knows you better than you know yourself, at other times doesn't understand you at all. He even makes fun of your dreams.

The basic principles that have been discussed throughout this book can be used with any difficult man, no matter what his relationship to you. Clara used what she had learned at home with her difficult fiancé in the office with her difficult boss.

Bob is Clara's husband. He's a successful executive in the oil industry, where he's well respected and wields authority. But he sometimes expects his authority to be as unquestioned at home as in the office. He has criticized Clara in front of others when she disagrees with him, and often neglects to ask for her input on family decisions. Over the years Clara has become increasingly angry about this, especially now, since she has achieved her own success as a stockbroker, and sees that she's accorded more respect at work than at home. Clara worked on her and Bob's problem with new confidence, and Bob has learned to save his critiques of her until they are alone. He consults with her more than he used to about plans and decisions. Overall, Clara feels better about their relationship in the past year than she did for the six years before that. Bob has always been supportive of her career and she admires his intelligence.

Coincidentally, Clara's new boss at work has a lot in common with Bob. He needs to be right and in charge all the time, criticizes her at meetings, and neglects to get her opinion when he's asking her male colleagues for theirs. He does think she's very skillful and tells her so. However, Clara feels more scared about talking to her boss than to Bob. Despite her fear, when he shut her up at the last meeting, she decided she had had enough. After the meeting Clara stopped in to see her boss. She first made a supportive comment. "I thought your idea about how to advertise to retired people was great." She then firmly but calmly said, "You've been criticizing my ideas and shutting me up at the last few meetings, and I resent you for it. I enjoy working for you, but this is going to interfere with our relationship if it continues. I want to hear what you have to say when we disagree, but not like this. It makes both of us look bad. Can you phrase your comments differently so as not to wipe me out?" Her boss was at first defensive and told her she was too sensitive. But he admitted that his wife had the same complaint. Most important, his destructive comments at the meetings ceased.

When Clara places her positive and negative statements together, she emphasizes her desire to improve the relationship. This communication strategy has worked before with her husband. Why shouldn't it succeed with her boss, also a difficult man, as well? As has been mentioned in previous chapters, all of us have a tendency to find a mate who will treat us in the way that we were treated by our parents. Thus, if your lover becomes cold and withdraws from you when he is angry, it is likely that your father (or mother) acted in the same way. The practice that you get in relating to your difficult lover can be used in dealing with your similar parent. For example,

Joan's father has a great sense of humor—all her friends agree. And he always sounds interested in Joan's latest artistic endeavors—most recently sculpture classes.

But he upsets Joan when he asks anxiety-provoking questions and avoids her entirely for periods of time. Most recently, Joan exhibited some of her work at a public library. True to form, Joan's father asked lots of questions about theft and insurance, what kind of money she would make from this, and why the library was interested in her "stuff." Because Joan's boyfriend, Ted, had made her anxious with the same kinds of questions, Joan was prepared for her father. She asked him, "How am I supposed to feel when you make comments like that? Should I get anxious and upset like you?" Lateness is another trait that Ted and her father share. After Joan finally refused to meet Ted anywhere, rather than wait for him, he started being on time. At the opening of her sculpture exhibit, however, Joan's father was not only late—he never made it at all. Because Joan was familiar with this problem with Ted, she was ready to speak up directly to her father later that night. "I'm really upset that you didn't make it after you said you would. It feels as if you don't care about my work when you don't show up. Can you tell me that you're proud of me and that you do feel good about the exhibit?" Joan's father was able to respond positively to this.

Joan did not develop the ability to communicate in this way overnight. During the months and years that she worked on the relationship with Ted, she became expert in taking the calculated emotional risks that are so necessary when loving a difficult man. She assessed that her father was twin, in some ways, to Ted. Both men she loved and hated at times. She realized that she would have to be the one to work on the relationship with her father, just as she had been with Ted, because her father would never assume the responsibility.

Many of the women I have worked with are family caretakers. They naturally give more than they get back to everyone in the family. Often a difficult brother is the biggest taker. The same concepts and tactics that you use in relating to your mate —asking for nurturance, taking care of him less unless he takes care of you more, identifying the problem and your feelings about it, even carefully considered and worded ultimatums— can be used with a sometimes selfish or self-centered brother.

But in the long run there is more that you can gain from taking emotional risks with all these difficult men than just an improved relationship. Whether or not your man, whoever he is, eventually responds in the ways that you wish, your psychological self will be enhanced in several ways:

1. You develop self-awareness. Gradually you will know what you feel at the very moment of a difficult situation instead of never knowing or becoming aware days or even years later.

2. You have the additional advantage of knowing what the psychological reasons are for your behavior and the other person's. Knowledge is power.

3. You become aware of what you need from others in relationships, and who is most likely to be giving.

4. You develop confidence in your feelings and intuition, and learn to love your emotional self in all its variations.

5. You broaden your skills in being able to deal with difficult people wherever and whenever you may meet them.

Thus you can see that in the process of loving a difficult man —which means giving him and the relationship the chance to improve through your efforts—you can become a more confident, self-defined, and self-realized woman. Just how you do this has been explained in these chapters, but let's review the main how-tos of loving your difficult mate.

A Review of the How-Tos

The essential qualities for loving a difficult man are courage and confidence. You'll need them as you take emotional risks and delve into the taboo problem areas. The first risk in loving a difficult man is to take a firm stand about the need for a monogamous commitment. Although this sounds simple, when you make a request for monogamy you are taking the biggest risk of all. A minor danger is that your man will be angry, feel controlled. But more terrifying is that he may minimize your importance to him, deny that he ever felt "that way" about you, and threaten to end the relationship, or actually pull out. Without a monogamous commitment, there is no possibility that your relationship can grow more intimate and trusting, or that it can be the secure base from which you venture forth to succeed in life.

Simultaneously develop awareness of your inner feeling life and respect for the feelings you uncover. When your feelings escape you, try to determine why this occurs. Are you afraid to know what you feel? Be patient with yourself. Developing full awareness of your feelings can take years, and requires constant vigilance. Once you have some idea of what you feel, you can use these feelings to help you guide the relationship toward intimacy. When the most powerful of these feelings—

anger, frustration, jealousy, warmth, and love—occur, you should interpret them as indications of what you want and don't want from him, how you do or don't want to be treated. Become aware of what upsets you and what pleases you based on your feeling reaction.

Equally important, search out the psychological reasons from both of your pasts that contribute to your behavior now. Whether the issue is money or sex, family visits or vacation plans, try to understand the causes rather than automatically placing blame on him or on yourself. Remember that you are always entitled to feel upset or angry about anything that takes place between you even if he is "right." When your feelings seem too intense or even out of control, pinpoint the incidents from your childhood that are adding extra emotional weight. Write down what you feel, speak to friends or to a therapist to get support and understanding. But no matter what, never let your feelings pile up inside. Assess whether you are an "over-complainer" or a "silent sufferer." You may need to hold back your feelings periodically or let them out more often.

In as caring a manner that you can develop (don't try to be an angel—you're only human), take an emotional risk and bring up the problems that are troubling you. If you feel apologetic, embarrassed, or scared, you are blaming yourself for your troubles and this will sabotage your struggle to get him to hear you. Determine why you might feel you don't deserve more in a relationship. The more confident you are that you deserve to be treated better, the more likely that your man will respond. A three-part communication like this one has the best chance of getting results:

1. State the problem.

2. Express your feelings about the problem.

3. Suggest how to alleviate the problem or request what you want from him.

Affection, warmth, love, appreciation, admiration, and praise should be expressed in equal proportions to anger and frustration about the problems. Holding back on nurturance can be destructive to your efforts to get what you want from the man in your life. Make it clear to him that you need to be nurtured in return.

A difficult man can be emotionally explosive or withholding, outright demanding or depriving through passivity. He can punish you with silence or hurt you with verbal abuse. Although you want to make a strong effort to improve the relationship rather than give up or resign yourself to a life of misery, you must also protect yourself from becoming burnt out through your labors. Take care of yourself both physically and emotionally by choosing supportive friends and rewarding activities. Your exercise, diet, satisfying artistic and creative endeavors, must all take priority to "working on" the relationship. If you wait for him to make you feel good without looking elsewhere, you may have a long wait and starve emotionally in the meantime.

And lastly, two of the general points bear repeating.

1. Difficult men disown their own upsetting feelings. Since you are a sensitive woman, you may unconsciously start to "own" what he has disowned, feel anger that is really his, anxiety and fear that he doesn't want. If you are overloaded with feelings while he expresses none, be aware that you are carrying a double burden, and use the

various techniques described in Chapter 8 to unload on him what is rightfully his.

2. Never make decisions, plans, or strategies when you are caught up in a torrent of anger. Anger passes quickly. When you are calm, use your intelligence, common sense, and insight to instruct you.

Survival Techniques—Being Separate

Difficult men do not think they are difficult until a woman tells them so. So, unfortunately, the job of improving your relationship falls in your lap. What can you do to survive the frustration of living with a difficult man when the messages are not getting through? The following survival techniques will assist you through these frustrating moments because they are meant to help you become more separate. As a separate individual, you'll need less from him, and there's a better chance that you'll feel less disappointed when he refuses to hear you for periods of time. There are some difficult men, though not all, who will at least temporarily become more giving when their woman becomes more separate from them. But use these survival techniques for yourself, not in order to "get something" from him.

1. Whether you yearn to sing or climb mountains, it is important that you *pursue your separate interests* while you are with your difficult man. Since difficult men often criticize your separate activities because of their insecure feelings, find others to encourage you. If you are still

paralyzed, then you have made your mate into an authority figure from your past and have invested his approval or disapproval with far too much power over your happiness and self-image. You will tend to repeat this pattern with any man in your life until you take a risk of living your own life while you are still with him. The rewards are: feeling happier and satisfied with yourself even though he is depriving you, and realizing that you can survive despite his disapproval.

2. You need to build a wall between yourself and his problems, just low enough so you can look over and know what his problems are, but high enough to stop you from taking responsibility from them. Women often feel guilty, even heartless, when they let him wrestle with his own problems and don't rush in to solve the difficulties he has created for himself. But it is really far crueler to take on his problems as your own because it prevents him from maturing and growing. What therapists call "differentiating" means defining the difference between you and those you love. Differentiation is a necessary step toward finding fulfillment in life. *Take no responsibility for his difficulties* and you will both benefit.

3. Another way to feel separate from the man in your life is to *occasionally hold back your emotional reactions,* especially when you feel intensely angry, frustrated, depressed, or anxious. Of course, this is not easy to do. If being angry, for instance, has become a habit for you and for him, hold back your feelings and expect to feel lonely and distant, even depressed. However, you will suddenly have more emotional room to reflect on what is happening between you, what being separate from

242

him feels like, and whether fear of this separateness is the only tie binding you to him. Are there traits of his that you still find lovable (when he's not being difficult) or are you with him because you are afraid to be alone?

4. Many of my women patients feel scared when they *imagine breaking up.* Others enjoy fantasizing about what it would be like to be single again or for the first time, to live alone or meet new men, or manage financially. This exercise—fantasizing—helps you develop the confidence to live without your man. Surprisingly, this confidence in your ability to be alone is helpful not only for your growth, but for the future of the relationship. You will be less afraid to know what you feel and ask for what you need when you realize you can live without him. Often women refuse to imagine their lives without their man because the terror of being alone (known as a separation anxiety) overwhelms them. This terror originates in childhood. Therapy can help you feel more confident as a separate individual if you are paralyzed by separation fears. Confidence in your separate self strengthens love as Han Suyin, a Chinese writer, stated. ". . . love from one being to another can only be that two solitudes come nearer, recognize and protect and comfort each other."

5. The last way to take care of yourself and feel more separate is to convince your man and yourself to *go for couples therapy.* It is the place of last resort to try to save a relationship before you call it quits. Men who are openly belligerent and nasty or quietly destructive cannot be loving and cooperative because of strong feelings of vulnerability. Even these "macho men" who are

"therapy haters," however, do profit from couples therapy because deep down they feel protected by an objective third person, less vulnerable, and thus do not have to keep their woman at a distance physically and emotionally. You can let the third person do some of the work, then, so that your time and energy can be spent more on you. If you do pursue couples therapy (also known as marital therapy, family therapy, conjoint counseling), the test of the right therapist for you as a couple is that each of you feels understood by the professional you choose.

Difficult men—on the one hand, explosive, silent, controlling, withholding, self-centered, arrogant; on the other, sensitive, helpful, charming, talented, or funny—in whatever variety, have filled your life since the day you were born. All men are difficult, some more so than others. Perhaps the key to loving such a man is to be well armed psychologically (to understand why he does what he does), to maintain a vision of the improved relationship you want and confidence in your feelings and intuition that will direct your efforts toward that future relationship. And to be willing to take an emotional risk when necessary. On the road to loving and understanding him and getting what you want, you should come to understand and love yourself as well. That is the secret to loving a difficult man.